The Science of Science

&

The Science of Life

(1970)

*

Traumear

Paperback ISBN 978-0-244-18852-8

*

www.traumear.com

Index

*

The Science of Science

The understanding makes theorems and arrives at distinctions.

Theorems are either extrinsic, when they are substantial, or else intrinsic, when they are reflective. Distinctions are arrived at either in reference to the understanding or else with respect to that which is to be understood.

*

Experiment

The understanding shapes theorems or it forms concepts.

Theorems are either extrinsic or intrinsic to the understanding.

Concepts are formed inherently or in conjunction with theorems.

Concepts inherent to the understanding are substantial, and those formed in conjunction with theorems are reflective.

*

Theorems embody substance. They are substance incarnate.

Concepts connect the understanding with the imagination, with which it is one, or else they establish a contact between the two.

Extrinsic theorems embody reflected substance, intrinsic theorems embody pure substance.

Concepts inherent to the understanding connect it with the imagination, and concept which are formed in conjunction with theorems establish a contact between the two.

*

The understanding and the imagination are one because of their connection and contiguity through concepts.

Cause transcends effect.

Effect precedes cause, and proceeds from it.

Every process is preceded by a concept.

*

Memory is an adjunct of the understanding

The source of memory is shape or form. It springs from one or the other, spontaneously, as an occurrence, or intentionally, as a process.

The origin of memory is either a theorem or a concept. It arises spontaneously from the former by association and intentionally from the latter as recall.

Association and recall are the two ways of memory.

———

2

of things:

Whatever can be scientifically known and understood is either organized or created.

Creation renders substance discernible. Organization allows it to become useful.

Created things have characteristics, by means of which they respond and relate. Organized things have properties, through which they correspond and correlate. Characteristics reveal what a thing is made of. Properties show how a thing works. Created things are either creations or creatures. Creations relate by means of such characteristics which flow freely from their being. A creation cannot be distinguished or set apart from its characteristics, but it is what they are. Each characteristic is a detail which shows the whole being of the entire reaction, and nothing else which pertains to the reaction may be had outside of it.

Creations respond by means of such characteristics which reflect spontaneously their being. Response entails reflection, and every reflection pertaining to the creation gives evidence of and bears testimony to the whole being of the creation and in short proves it.

A creature relates and responds by means of characteristics which have been acquired. They are either acquired in such a way that the creature becomes one with them or else they are adopted. In the former case the characteristics reveal to us both the relative origin or genus of the creature and its inherent purpose or destiny, which is called species. In the case of adopted characteristics one relies on an interpretation of these characteristics to point to the manner of being or behaviour of the creature, and from this behaviour an understanding of the creature is deduced. Its genus is then discovered by means of analogy to other creatures of the same type, and its species may be divined from the genus.

Organized things are either organs, organisms or organizations. An organ has a use. It uses up substance and produces something. The connection between the substance and the product can never be found out and always takes us to the organ itself. An organism makes use of things. It assimilates them and turns them into its own substance or else it uses them in order to make use of other things. It is its own product. While organs are simply named, organisms are classified according to the purpose they serve. Organizations are useful. They are made use of by other things and have no purpose of their own but are a purpose in themselves. They are organized for the sake of something else with which they become one. An organization unifies while an organ brings about a duality.

*

of the understanding:

To understand means to be one and to become one with substance.

To know means to be one and to become one with reality.

The universe, which is reality, is made up of one single substance.

Nothing can be outside the universe.

The universe is identical with the substance which it is made up of. There is nothing which is completely without knowledge or entirely incapable of understanding, since everything must at least be something, even if it does not become something, and therefore, since it cannot be outside of the universe, it is one with the universe, which means that it knows, and similarly it is one with substance, which means that it understands.

Being is the embodiment of substance, or incarnation.

To become something means to take on its form, its shape and its size, in that order and all inclusively.

Form, shape and size are the three categories or classes of substance.

Outside of form, shape and size, substance cannot be purely conceived. Neither can it be purely conceived in any one of these separate and distinct from the others, nor in any two of them alone, but in all three is substance understood and known if it is conceived purely.

When we turn away entirely from understood things and confront the understanding itself, we come upon memory, intelligence and fantasy. They are pure human form, human shape and human size. These are the three categories or classes of thought, which is pure human substance.

*

of things:

Correspondence and correlation of organized things through their properties involves the world. The world is a created thing. The earth is also a created thing, but it is a creature, while the world is a creation. The correspondence of organized things through their properties inhabits the earth and the correlation of organized things through their properties orders it.

The names of all created things and the number of them which occurs give us the first indication of how they should be conceived of. Whatever creature or creation does not yet have a name must be given one. These names are all taken for granted. When we are in possession of the name of a created thing, we are in possession of that thing itself. (In order to come into possession of it we need merely to believe that this is true, as has been amply proven in the foregoing philosophy.) The total number of created things does not change. What this number is, is not of the least importance, but only that it does not ever change. What changes is the number of particular created things of a certain given name. Once we now this number and are in possession of the created thing's name, we are able to deduce from this the thing's position and location in the universe as a result of that information, and since we understand the universe as a whole, we are able to understand the particular created thing in the universe as an individual.

The number of organized things is not constant. Organized things do not have names, but they are referred to within a scheme of classification. This is a proper scheme of classification, because it contains only those things, organized things, to which classification has been judged to be not inappropriate. Before we begin to classify however we must show clearly how organs, organisms and organizations differ from each other according to the properties through which they correspond and correlate.

The properties of an organism allow it to cope autonomously in an environment. This is another way of saying that an organism behaves. Neither organs nor organizations behave. Behaviour entails an awareness simultaneously of oneself and of one's surroundings. Out of this awareness springs first of all the creative impulse, which is the wish to imitate oneself and one's surroundings and to make them the same. The three properties required in order to succeed in this are authenticity, authority and control.

*

of the understanding:

Turning again to the understanding we find ourselves confronted by realization, recognition and thought. They are the three basic human functions. Whatever is substantial therefore may be realized, recognized or thought, depending not on any quality or attribute of the substance, but only on human decision.

Our understanding is not based on anything else. The human functions above mentioned contribute to the understanding without themselves becoming involved in it. Hence we speak of free thought, of immediate recognition and of true realization. Each of these functions is capable correspondingly of thinking, recognizing and realizing itself. Thought thinking itself is the idea. Recognition recognizing itself is the notion, and realization realizing itself is the mind. The results of the reflexive functions: idea, notion and mind, have their counterparts when the three functions work spontaneously. They are the word in the case of thought, speech in the case of recognition, and in the case of realisation – language.

An attribute compares to a function as reason compares to consciousness. The three human attributes are mastery, personality and eternity. It is through the understanding that these attributes are attained; without the understanding they cannot be retained. We do not know what it means to be human until we understand these attributes and consequently are in their possession. Separately and distinctly they cannot be had, but only all three together.

The attributes of the understanding itself which make it a human understanding are lust, individuality and purpose. Again they cannot be separated. Where and whenever they do occur separately they are not good. As a whole they are holy.

Lust is that inordinate desire of the human being to understand not some or many, but specifically all things. Only as an attribute of the understanding however and consequently in link with the other two attributes mentioned above can lust be a good thing, when it desires also to understand itself and succeeds in this.

When the human understanding cannot be analyzed any further, when nothing else can be abstracted from it and when all its physical parts or members have become insolubly attached through sufficient memory work, then the understanding possesses individuality. Any individuality which does not at least stem from this individuality of the understanding is merely hypothetical and has no real value. The individuality of our understanding, once it has been achieved, allows us to see our-

7

selves as we truly are, at the centre of the universe and absolutely indestructible.

The perfection of the understanding also presupposes that it has a purpose. This purpose must be single, simple and unique. Every human being is capable of possessing such a purpose.

Its singularity excludes all perversion and aberration of body and soul. Since only one purpose is posited, the way must be straight, whether it is a way of knowing or a way of behaving

The simplicity of the purpose disallows all extraordinary and abnormal interests which do not serve this good purpose immediately and directly, and it advances only such deeds which must not first be interpreted in the light of something else before they may be justified, but which stand on their own merits and are therefore in no need of prior or consequent justification.

It is its simplicity of purpose which gives the understanding its special ability of divination. This is not difficult to comprehend when we reflect upon our understanding of the universe as a created thing whether a thing is divinely or humanly created does not make one whit of difference since the act of creation is the same no matter who performs it (provided we understand passion as an activity, not as something contrary to it). Divination is possible on the basis of the knowledge of divine and human collaboration in the creative act, not as it once came about, but as it happens now and will happen ever after. We must only decide whether we wish to accept or to reject the new covenant, which is a perfect agreement of reality with the truth in its fullness. An acceptance persuades us of the simplicity of the universal purpose, within which our own then resides. Consequently we may see and act upon even the innermost meaning and intent of reality itself as it is and exists. This we call divination.

A purpose is unique when it is expressible both in particular and in general terms, and no less easily in one than in the other.

For example if our purpose is expression itself, then this purpose will be unique if we can find nothing to express in the real universe which does not at the same time and to the same degree impress itself upon our imagination on the basis of our understanding. A cloud for instance will exist both here and there. Our friend will be equally important for us, though in a different way perhaps, whether he is dead or alive, and as far as our understanding is concerned, we will know that we are in the possession of it whether we are aware of its affects or not. The difference between the relative and the absolute has dwindled to the point where its consideration for the sake of life has become pointless. Consequently we do not bother to take account of it but simply strive in earnest to such a degree that our emotions and thoughts, our pains and sensations all point to that one source of life to which we address ourselves and come to focus on its ultimate identification with our person. At such a stage of being we automatically refrain from any criticism; our judgment is entirely self-oriented. Since all things here point to us, we can do no wrong, and may simply act as our understanding desires of us. But much preparation is required before such a stage is reached, and so that no presumption or premature activity may interfere with the ultimate plan of all reality, its secrets are carefully guarded against unclean intrusion – on one hand by the love of knowledge, which must be borne and undergone like a test and then faithfully requited, and on the other hand by the love of our fellow man, fallible like us and at all times capable of perfection. In the private domain of our mind, we must meet the same standard of perfection as in the public realm of human society as it is, not as we wish it to be, if we are ever to be allowed past the cherubim through the gates into our paradise.

of things:

Organs do not behave, like organisms, but they work. We have spoken of input and of output in the case of organs, and of the impossibility of establishing a link between the two except as the organ itself. This does away with the problem of reflective action, as we shall soon come to see more clearly.

The work which an organ does is either purposeful or else mechanical. The latter we may refer to as labour, but the former cannot be given another name because we cannot do it and refer to it at the same time.

Purposeful work results in a product which has value of its own, while labour simply contributes to a change of appearances.

Mechanical work, such as any machine is capable of, defines the organ which produces it and limits it so that it may have meaning and so that it may exist. Combine harvesters and computers are organs only while they are in operation and not while they sit idle. Farmers and mathematicians are organs while the one farms and the other mathematizes. Their labour defines them, since without it they must be some other thing, organic or not, and it limits them, in that without it they cannot be what they have become.

All work incorporates the law. Outside of work and of works there is no law. Work incorporates the law progressively and a work incorporates it statically. To incorporate means to embody as a whole.

The law does not primarily rule or regulate but it institutes. Every institution of the law is either right or just. Whatever has a right, to do or to be or whatever, differs from that which is just in that it cannot contain the law except as an indication of its own behaviour; it is lawful in that it behaves lawfully, whereas a just thing, insofar as we regard it for the sake of discovering this, contains the law also in that it fulfils it. The just thing is lawful whether it behaves or not, but when a thing must behave in order to be lawful, then it cannot be said to be just, but it has the right to behave in one manner of another.

Right institutions and just institutions of the law have this in common, that they institute the law and, which is the same, that the law institutes them. The institution of the law can be understood both as an imprint of a general thing on a particular one, in a peculiar fashion of course, and as the incarnation of a general thing by a particular one, in a peculiar fashion. We need not disturb ourselves about the peculiarity of the way in which this imprint or that incarnation comes about. Such an endeavour is at worst self-abusive and at best perfectly useless. What concerns us alone are the ways in which this institution of the law may be understood, so that we may proceed to understand it.

Only one particular institution of the law is required so that all things may be both lawful and just. We are able today to understand the necessary prerequisites of such an institution. We have shown elsewhere that the earth is the centre of the universe and that man is its master. We have also learned only recently above that a being is human if it possesses at once the three attributes of mastery, personality and eternity. That particular institution of the law which fulfils all things would have to be located centrally so that no thing is removed from it any further than another, and so that it would be equally available to all things with respect to order and justice. Whether we imagine this centrality of location, as an analogy to our understanding, or whether we perceive it distinctly, we can see how it is a necessary prerequisite for the institution under our consideration, and how it is good that the earth takes in such a position with respect to the rest of the universe. Now if an institution of the law is to be of a sovereign nature and all-inclusive, and since man is by definition master of the universe, it stands plainly to reason that such an institution should come about and take place through human means rather than through any other. So much for the justice of this institution: where it should take place and through what means.

It is to be its nature that it fulfil all things with respect to the law. If it should turn out now that the attributes of human nature are such that the institution of the law through them could indeed proceed in such a way that all things be fulfilled, then we might well yearn, insofar as we have human understanding, that such an institution become an actual fact.

Personality allows the assimilation of all things. Only one thing is common to all things, and that is that they may be perceived by a person on this plane or, more accurately, in this manner, through personal perception, all things may become one and similarly accessible. In short, they may all be assimilated.

Mastery is responsible for the alignment and ordering of all things for one singular purpose, and for their understanding in the light of that same purpose. A unique action is masterful in this way, and we think of it as creative.

Eternity is possessed and given by a thing which lasts. It does not predetermine change, but change is rendered constant by it, so that the eternal thing changes absolutely with respect to itself and the universe, and relatively with respect not to some, but to all things other than itself. (With respect to the universe, of course, the difference between absolute and relative has very little meaning.)

Fulfilment according to the law means primarily the embodiment of the law in such a way that no aspect of the law remains outside of the thing under consideration. It must contain the whole law as it is embodied in the universe; corporeal, physically accessible and intrinsic. We describe this embodiment in terms of the word.

Secondarily fulfilment according to the law means that no basis of foundation is required outside of the fulfilled thing so that it may live. Whatever basis one postulates, one knows that the postulate must either add to or take away from the thing under consideration for which one desires the foundation, and one understands that the fulfilled thing cannot be hypothetically approached for any useful purpose. We speak here of the fulfilled thing's integrity.

Finally, if a thing is to be fulfilled according to the law, it must fit perfectly into its environment. This is a matter of the present time, not of the past or of the future. But we know that the present time is not another thing like the past and the future or somehow in the same category with it or extrapolatable from a same common denominator, bur that it inculcates the future and the past, rendering them also somehow present, through such devices as memory, recall, providence, prediction etc.

Consequently for a thing to fit perfectly into its environment it must be independent of a mere past or future and it must be eternal. Human nature is able to provide this as we have shown. The assimilation of this aspect of human nature proceeds by way of personality and the necessary integrity of the fulfilled thing is brought about by the mastery of human nature which is able to conceive things as integral and as absolutely purposeful. The theoretical construct of every thing may then be abandoned, and the total embodiment of the law occurs as a result of expression, which may happen in an infinite variety of ways, as it in reality does. Only language however, through the human organ of speech, is able to assign the word in such a way that a thing is actually touched, in its being, and only human language as speech can designate the universe and all things in it in such a manner, that nothing remains to be understood.

*

of the understanding:

That part of the understanding which is especially suited to inquiry into matters and problems of law and which is in itself a manifestation of that same law, is the judgment. It is not a faculty nor an attribute. Metaphorically judgment is a confrontation of the law with itself.

For judgment to happen, a real thing must be available to be judged. Without this, judgment is to a degree perverse and to that degree accompanied and inhibited by guilt.

Once judgment has achieved the status of reality, it can turn towards itself. Judgment judging itself is called divine judgment, and also the last judgment, since beyond this no higher judgment can be attained to. We cannot talk about it therefore without being hypocritical, and can only give an example of it, thereby demonstrating its attributes.

Let our will be the thing which is judged first, as part of the judgment. It becomes divided consequently into conscience and intellect. This division is necessary so that an estimation according to the law of the thing under scrutiny may proceed. Each of the resulting parts of this division, halves with respect to their prejudged entity but in their own right entities in themselves, may again be divided in the same way, and so on until a satisfactory degree of evidence has been gained. Conscience, in our example, divides into consciousness and knowledge, while the intellect divides into emotion and awareness. The evidence gained in this case allows us to discriminate.

Discrimination, like simple division, is an attribute of real judgment. When a real thing has been divided in the manner above into its two essential components, then we are able justly to discriminate between the two, however in a peculiar fashion. We may not rely on a common basis of the two components. Neither are we allowed to presuppose a hypothetical or theoretical link between the two which might or might not reveal itself as true or practicable during inquiry. Instead, discrimination spontaneously makes obvious certain similarities and differences between the components without supplying any reason for these which is not self-evident.

One of the two components which results from an act of discrimination is always inferior and the other is always superior. Inferior and superior may refer to qualities, but this is a matter of application, not of necessity. It happens most commonly in the case of discrimination that the usual is confused with the good. Inferior and superior are not kinds of quality or types of quantity nor do they have any third thing in common, but they are attributes generally of judgment and more specifically of discrimination. As such they both infer pure substance, inferior judgment directly and superior judgment or superior discrimination indirectly. Intellect for example is the inferior of the two components of the will and as such it lends itself to inferior judgment. This means that substance becomes available through it in such a way that the understanding is able to manipulate what it deals with without first having to seek or construct a rational basis on which to found its conclusions. From an inferior thing the understanding concludes immediately, judgment proceeds directly and discrimination likewise.

The special capacity of judgment is discernment. Once the inferior component of a real thing has been discriminated from the superior one, such as intellect from conscience in the case of the will and awareness from knowledge in the case of the intellect, one may discern how it is inferior or superior, or more precisely, how it comes to be as it is. The way is pointed out when we understand it to be inferior or superior, and subsequently it may be described accurately by means of discernment.

Knowledge for example, the superior one of the two components of the conscience, may be discerned to be an aggregate of information and a summation of learned data. These are not components as in the case of discrimination, but together they bring us into contact with the elements of reality as they appear in their eightfold pattern. Discernment differentiates the two associated groups of this pattern, information and data in our present example, and on top of this it gives us an infallible indication of the specific nature of each group, so that we know in our example that the information is available as an aggregate, and that the data are in addition and learned.

15

Finally it is decision which breaks down a real thing into its last components or particular elements. Of the intellect it is awareness which is the inferior component. (We remind again that inferiority and superiority are attributes of discrimination and not of the real thing itself.) Awareness then makes substance available directly and emotion makes it available indirectly. The indirect means in the case of the substantiation of emotion is rational control through love.

We discern that emotion, insofar as it is controlled by love of course, is active passion and certain feeling. These two groups of emotion may be described as they appear in the typical eightfold pattern, and we decide finally, as the ultimate stage of that part of the understanding which is judgment, that the four active passions are care, hope, honour and dignity; and that the four certain feelings which make up the other group of the eight elemental emotions are certainty, constancy, continuity and consequence.

It is important to keep in mind here that these eight elemental emotions, instead of being treated as real things in themselves as we choose to do, can also be divested of their substance, in which case the active passions become mental and hypothetical virtues and the certain feelings become theoretical concepts and terms. As such they have their value. Once we have made contact with reality however, that is to say with real things, and once we are able to participate in its substance through the creative act and to partake of it in our understanding, we would be foolish ever to do without this gain. And so it happens even in fact that as we more and more become incarnate beings, whose body represents the soul rather than each one separately containing one, so are we less and less able to conceive of reality in theory and to construct it on hypothetical grounds, until finally we turn our ambition entirely away from such endeavours and train it wholly on that reality which is what it is and becomes as it will be.

*

of things:

Organizations are composed of parts. Each part of the organization is a detail of the whole. Every organization is a detail of the universe.

The detail is different in every respect from that of which it is a detail, and it has nothing in common with it. One detail of a whole is similar to every other detail of that same whole but it can never be the same. All the details of the same whole have one thing only in common, which is their entailment. They all entail the same concept.

The entailment of the various details and the concept which is entailed by them is not the same thing. The difference lies in this, that the detail derives wholeness through its entailment but unity from the concept which it entails. Whatever is whole and also has unity necessarily varies. This means that it is not exactly the same as any other thing.

Varying things are either details or organizations of varieties.

Details vary in comparison to their organization and in comparison to the other details of the same organization taken one, several or all at a time.

In comparison to their organization, details vary entirely. This means that they have nothing in common with them and that they are similar to them in one, in several, or in all ways.

Similarity is due to association. It is strictly a matter of appearance. When things are similar they seem to have one or more things in common, but in fact, in truth and in reality they do not. Association assimilates and it is through this assimilation that things can become perfectly alike in appearance. When no difference of appearance can be detected in things then we may say that they share equally in one and the same appearance but they cannot be said to have a particular appearance in common because appearance cannot be possessed. What matters here again and is of utmost importance is that we differentiate

17

concisely between substance, which is really possessed, and motion, which is not really possessed, but only perhaps in a manner of speaking.

In comparison to each other the details of the same organization vary not entirely, but essentially. This means that they exist in the same way but in a different manner. An analogy is required to illustrate this difference, on one hand between the way and the manner, and on the other hand between various manners. The way in which a thing exists pertains to its purpose, but the manner in which it exists pertains to its end. An animal may gather food in order to survive and for the sake of enjoyment. Another animal may gather food in order to survive and for the sake of nourishment.. the two animals, to the extent of this example, exist in a different manner in that they survive differently, one through the enjoyment of food and the other by means of its nourishment but they exist in the same way, not in that they both gather food in order to survive which is their reason for existing, nor in that they both gather food, which is their reason for survival, (since there is no such thing in reality as a will or a drive or a desire to live, and therefore, within the bounds of our analogy, if the animals were prevented from gathering food, then they would die not because they have no food but because they have no more reason to live) but in that both of them behave. That they behave in a similar fashion, by gathering food, is simply an accident of the analogy, and that they both are animals is a coincidence of the chosen example. We might as well have chosen an animal and a human being and we might have had one of them gathering food and the other expending its energy. The analogy would have been less plain and the example less clear, but both things might still have existed in the same way in that, for the sake of the argument, they behaved, and in a different manner, in that, for the sake of discussion, one of them enjoyed its food, for whatever reason, and the other nourished itself by means of it.

Organisations vary in accordance with their detailed composition, which is called variance, and with respect to teach other, which is called variation.

Variance arises out of the way in which the various details of an organization associate. This association may occur usually (which includes the unusual), normally (which includes the abnormal) or legally (which includes the illegal).

Usual association assimilates the various details of an organization in such a way that they seem to be similar in truth. The outcome of such an association is a likely truth or a truthful likeness. The portrait of a woman for example is likely true if it reminds us of her personality or of a particular person at all and attaches us to this by means of form, shape and size. Particular cases are to be found among the works of the cubist painters. A portrait of a woman is a truthful likeness however if appearances are observed according to an accepted standard and we are encouraged to identify with those appearances through the treatment of our senses due to motion, rest and energy. Photography offers the most striking cases of truthful likeness. Others may be found among paintings by Andrew Wyeth.

Normal association assimilates the various details of an organization in such a way that they seem to be similar in fact. Where the apparent similarity in truth of its parts allowed an organization to vary according to a polarity arrangement of its elements, between truthful likeness and likely truth, so does the apparent similarity in fact allow variance according to a diagrammatic arrangement of its elements. This means that a two-dimensional figure is able fully to represent the organization's associated composition. The two dimensions may be any of an infinite number of possible ones, but they must be taken from within the association of detail, and may not be imprinted upon it from without. Let us presume for the sake of explanation that a certain factory manufactures things from wood. As an organization its various detailed parts might be the preparation of trees

19

for cutting, the upkeep of pertinent machinery, the marketing of its finished product, the distribution of financial profit and perhaps the construction of barrels. Reviewing what is at stake here we understand: 1.) that this organization varies in accordance with the association of its various details; 2.) that its variance is normal, which means that the assimilation of its various parts, which is due to their association, occurs apparently in fact rather than apparently in truth or apparently in realty, and 3.) that this apparent similarity in fact stems from a diagrammatic arrangement of the thing's elements, which means that a two-dimensional figure can represent it fully. The two dimensions which we might choose for this, from within the association of detail, might possibly be the growth of the organization, in terms of manufacturing capacity and financial gain if we like, and its value as a factor contributing to the general and particular welfare of men. We then balance these two dimensions against each other, judge the result, and are left with an indication of the organization's special properties as a factory which manufactures barrels in a certain way.

This compares to the special properties of an organization with usual variance which were indicated to us above through the specific polarity arrangement of an organization's elements. The special properties through which the factory and the picture as organizations correspond (rather than correlate, since they vary in accordance with the association of their parts rather than with respect to other organizations) and through which they correspond not only to each other but even simply, might be probability of success, degree of virtual efficiency and actual potentiality in the case of the former and perhaps excitement, beauty and enjoyment in the case of the latter. In either case, since we are dealing with organizations, the results of our scientific inquiry will be useful.

The variance of an organization is legal when its detailed parts associate in terms of each other's existence. As a consequence these parts then seem to be similar in reality. A colony of ants might serve as an example of such an association, or a forest, or perhaps a human society which is not based on love but on law.

Of primary importance here is always the individuality of the association's every member. And of similar importance is this, that every one of these individuals has the same and an equal right. What this right is can never be finally and ultimately ascertained, except perhaps as the right to exist in one way or another, which is vague enough. But that is not important. What counts is that no individual has a greater right or more right than another.

An attempt to define an individual's right by deriving it from a description of his nature will not do, because its nature is neither preceded by its individuality nor is its individuality preceded by its nature. It is a mustard plant's nature to spring from a very tiny seed and then to extend its stems and branches very widely in proportion to the size of the seed. To say now that such a plant has a right to extend its leaves and branches so very widely in comparison to its beginning as a seed would be to beg the existential question. Since existence precedes essence, individuality is in itself a contrived thing, either derived from the reaction to an environment, or arrived at in reaction to an environment. In participation and collaboration with the environment there is no such thing as individuality.

Where a usual association of detail stemmed from a polarity arrangement of its elements, so does a legal association of detail stem from an extremity arrangement of its elements. The extremes are always expressed in legal terms and in terms of a specific law. The terms themselves must seem familiar, changing from situation to situation, from one second to the next and proverbially at the drop of a hat. But the law, even in its specific manifestations, does not change. "If the sun were to overstep his measure, the handmaids of justice would find him out."

21

The extremity arrangement of elements, which gives rise to a legal variance of organization, is in itself a definition of limits and of their possible extension. It need not be and cannot be defined again. Individuality is the limit of personal perception; right, or rights, are the limit of human understanding. When we project these extremes of our nature into an environment and then attempt stubbornly to dissociate ourselves from them, we soon begin to confound reality with its illusion and we are like the unfortunate clown who, on his day off decided finally to overcome gravity once and for all, so he leapt from the Golden Gate Bridge. On contemplating his death, he then discovered the real advantage of gravity.

Now that we have come to a clearer understanding of how organizations vary in accordance with the association of their detailed parts, which is called variance, we go on to show how they vary with respect to each other, which is called variation.

Every organization, when compared to any other organization, differs from it in at least one aspect. If two organizations were exactly the same the would be one and the same organization, which is an absurd consideration except insofar as it throws light on the nature of organization itself.

There is no such thing as a particular organization in itself. It must be viewed either in variance, compared to its similar parts, or else in variation, compared to another organization. The difference between various organizations arises out of their comparison to each other.

Comparison presupposes the simultaneous coexistence of two or more things. Such a coexistence is in fact the case, since all things do exist precisely at the same time, in the environment of realty. But in this environment we merely know that we coexist eternally with all other things, but we do not understand that it is so. In other words, in this environment we have eternal life but we do not understand what this means. We are not meant however merely to have pleasure, but also to enjoy our pleasure. Consequently we leave this environment and view it so to speak from the outside, and from within a particular environment, taking care not to confuse our state of being, which we freely choose, with our real existence and with our true life, which we wish more perfectly to understand.

Given this nature of comparison, we hold beside it the nature of organization, which is the bringing together of diverse pieces for the sake of a particular purpose or end. If our particular purpose is eternal life itself, or the coexistence with all other things in a real environment, then it is clear that the organization which we require for this is that of the world. The organization of the world makes available to us both a point of reference and a certain perspective which we may use and apply while we desire to understand our life insofar as it is eternal. This world cannot be of any use to us. However its organization makes available to us a standard of comparison according to which we may judge all life, both eternal and temporary.

Ever comparison necessarily begins with an encounter. The nature of an encounter is this, that two systems which are alike become one for a practical reason. Alike systems, as we remember from our philosophy, are either logical or psychosomatic or solar.

Organization can be defined as useful systems. Their systematic structure becomes apparent only when they are compared to each other. Since an encounter must occur if the comparison is to succeed, and since the systems which becomes one during the encounter must be alike, three different comparisons are possible.

Those organizations which compare psychosomatically vary in terms of their structure. Those organizations which compare logically vary in terms of their effects, and those which compare solarly, whose apparent structures are solar-systematic, vary in terms of their inherent effects or affects.

When we say that organizations vary in terms of their structure, of their effects or of their affects, we mean that the variation which exists is either structural, effectual or affectual, and that all variation must be approached on one of these three bases. Only in such a way can organizations be extrinsically understood, with respect to each other.

Before we discuss these three possible variations one at a time, we point out that variation and union are joint processes. One of them cannot be conceived in the absence of the other. An understanding of them can only be achieved if they are viewed simultaneously, as they happen. They depend upon each other for their mutual discernibility.

The variation of that organization whose structure is psychosomatic, in other words that variation which entails union with another psychosomatic structure and which is approached and viewed on the basis of structural rather than of effectual or affectual elements, allows that organization to be reborn. This means a complete change in form, shape and size.

The complete change in form is called transformation. It cannot come about in the absence of the other two, and all three changes, if they occur, must happen together. A complete change in shape is called metamorphosis, and a complete change in size is called transubstantiation. Rebirth is the ultimate success of all three changes and heralds that particular organization's fulfilment.

The actual rebirth of a structurally varying organization is fortuitous, which means that it can neither be mechanically prevented nor mechanically brought about. Also, and by the same token, although structural variation, like all variation, entails the union with the systematic structure of another organization, the actual rebirth of the one organization does not entail the rebirth of the other organization, with whose structure its own has become one. Organizations whose systematic structures have united are said to be adjacent, and their rebirths are independently fortuitous.

Now although this thing called rebirth happens fortuitously and cannot be mechanically prevented or brought about – which means that the cause does not include the effect – this is not to say that it happens accidentally, which would mean that the cause would exclude the effect, nor is it to say that it happens necessarily, which would mean that there would be neither cause nor effect but only a merely historical event, beyond judgment and repetition. In fact it may be prevented and brought about in every way and by all means which are to no degree and in nowise mechanical. Of course such ways and means cannot be given particular names, since any particular thing can be done to a degree or even completely mechanically, and therefore it must suffice to say that all ways and means which are not at all mechanical (which grants them a possible spontaneous nature) and from which every trace and vestige of mechanical pursuit has been removed (which grants the possibility of an achieved nature) may bring about or prevent such a rebirth. For the purpose of elaboration we emphasize what is already implicit in the foregoing, that an attempt at mechanical prevention might immediately precede the very thing which had been resisted and that, just as well, such an attempt to bring about a rebirth which had not been free of mechanical endeavour might also lead to rebirth, which could then be interpreted as miraculous and as exceptionally merciful, and would give a most trenchant evidence of the event's fortuitous nature. What cannot happen is that a totally mechanical pursuit, which can exist, might end in rebirth.

We have discussed how alike organizations, specifically those whose structure is psychosomatically systematic and which therefore vary in terms of their structure, vary in comparison to each other and upon encountering each other. Their variation approaches and perhaps results in rebirth and fulfilment, which means a complete change in form, shape and size.

If a rebirth actually succeeds, there can be, in the case of such an organization, no more question of individuality and right. A rebirth means that the law has been fulfilled, which means in turn that the very reason for the law's existence in the first place has in this particular instance of reality become null and void. The law, which exists for the sake of perfection and for the purpose of its ultimate achievement, does not any more support such an organization, not by any means, whether theoretical as in the case of hypothesis and precept, or practical as in the instance of method and technique, but instead the reborn organization embodies the law, which is the same law, but now unintelligible.

The question of course must arise as to what the reborn organization has in common, if anything, with ... but here words must fail us. If they did not, we would not have arrived at the point where we have presently arrived. Since we use language, and since language, as an organization, indeed at this point as the organization, cannot last except as an entity in itself, it is clear that we must, during the progress of our scientific endeavour, arrive at the ultimate and final limits of the representative and demonstrating word, at which time we cross the scientific river Styx on a bridge of metaphor, which is like the sign of equality by which the two sides of an equation are linked; (or at least should be linked, if we are dealing with a real and true equation.) The word is such a charming thing that we may employ it in order to represent, in fact, that of which it itself is the cornerstone. Or, to express the same more blithely, the word generates its own self. Consequently, since the word is always greater and more effective, which is to say more real, more perfect than whatever it stands for, there must come a time during our acquisition of knowledge for the sake of an understanding of real things, when no words are available to express this: that reality is what it is and nothing else. At such a time we make do with signs These signs, such as the familiar multiplication sign, or the comma at the end of a phrase, or a simple greeting to our neighbour, cannot be any further analyzed or described, since they all mean, though in a different setting, that reality is what it is, or, which is the same, that God is that he is.

The next task is to show how organizations vary if their systematic structure is logical rather than solar or psychosomatic.

The union of two logically systematic structures makes possible and facilitates the survival of both organizations which are being compared.

Survival is not a matter of life and death but of life or death. Whatever survives does not necessarily live, which is to say that its life does not include and overcome death, but it simply continues either to live or to die in the manner in which it lived or died previous to the comparative encounter. Whatever is truly alive may of course also survive by continuing to exist in the same manner as it exists in presently, and if it ceases to survive it does not necessarily stop living, although it may. But whatever must necessarily die if it does not survive was never truly alive but only merely so, and by the same token (or rather by the same lack of token, if science does not exclude humour) whatever cannot survive unless it continues living has in fact nothing to lose through its death, but only stands to gain by it. In conclusion, mere life survives or else succumbs to death, but real and true life may survive or not survive, but even if it succumbs it does not succumb entirely, but only in one manner or another, and always for the sake of more true life.

In short, survival does not mean the possession of true life but merely the retention of a manner or fashion of life.

Whatever survives is more fit than that which succumbs to it.

Fitness is entirely a matter of mechanical cause and effect. But since a cause is separate and distinct from its effect only to the degree that the two are connected other than mechanically (which implies what has been treated in our philosophy, namely

27

that the only true cause of an effect or of effects is entirely free and distinct from it and not at all mechanically connected) we need not concern ourselves at all with causes in the case of fitness, and may simply treat all those phenomena as effects.

Once the logically systematic structures of two varying organizations have joined, the two organizations are said to be identical.

Identical things are not the same, because although they do not differ from each other according to things other than themselves, they nevertheless differ with respect to each other. The difference lies in their essence.

Two identical organizations, which means two organizations whose structures are both logically systematic and one, are still related. This concept of relation has not yet been touched upon under these circumstances, but this will be done presently.

Organizations which do not vary are said to be neutral. As such they are all related, and in the following way. First of all it is important that their structures are all alike. Not until the organizations are compared to each other can their structures differ and become one. This throws light again on what it means to be one and united.

Whatever is not structured in an organization is a matter of influence and may be referred to in toto as the organization's sphere of influence, which is based on the concept of the field as it has been discussed in our philosophy. The spheres of influence of all neutral organizations are one and the same. In order now to understand what it means that all neutral organizations are related, and that they are totally related, we need simply to look at their dual construction, consisting of structure and a sphere of influence, and then in addition to this at what it means that all their structures are alike and that their spheres of influence are not alike but one and the same. Once we understand this relation we will be in a good position to understand those organizations which vary.

In the case of neutral organizations, the structure and the sphere of influence have nothing at all in common. We cannot even compare them negatively by saying that the former is structured and the latter is not, if we wish to preserve our absolute scientific accuracy, since a sphere of influence in the absence of a structure cannot be conceived. Neither can we say, therefore, that we are dealing with two parts of the same thing, since that would contradict the basic indivisibility of the organization and would negate its obvious visibility. A neutral organization is an individual thing. Now since the scientist may quarrel neither with what he sees nor with what he knows if he wishes sincerely to understand, he must rise finally to this reality of experience: he must rise to the occasion of what he truly experiences as reality, and he will admit and state that the structure of a neutral organization and the sphere of influence of a neutral organization are both real and incomparable. Therefore none of the infinite hair-splitting, which has been dogging us in the field of science while the imagination was not yet distinct and while thought consequently was not yet free, is required here. It does not happen that those things which bear the name of an indivisibility, such as an atom, do in fact come apart under our gaze, or that a sign, such as the two parallel dashes of the equal-sign, does not really stand for equality, but only denotes it or refers to it in connotation. It is the laborious processes of hypothesis and theory however which eventually free us even of themselves and allows a clear way for the true understanding of all that is real.

A thing is not a concept. It is therefore not contradictory or wrong to speak of incomparable things. If anyone wishes to coin thingness he is welcome to the small change. There is no room for it in the universe.

Incomparable things are simply that. Comparable things are alike, similar, the same, one or different.

The construction of two incomparable things, such as the structure and the influence of a neutral organization, is a special thing. All special things of the same order are referred to as a species. By the same order is meant that each incomparable thing must in each individual thing of the species stem from the same origin. By its origin again is meant the incomparable thing's existence in reference to space and time. So for instance we know that the incomparable structure of a neutral organization exists here and now, at the present time and immediately present, and that the incomparable sphere of influence of a neutral organization exists for all time, past, present and future, and everywhere, wherever there is space, whether that space is provided for it or else just happens to be where it is.

A species, for obvious reasons, cannot be re-categorized. When we say that a thing belongs to a certain species we have allocated it to its ultimate and archetypal order.

The species of neutral organizations, for example, cannot again be said to originate somewhere else or in another way. When we ask how and where a particular species originates, we must look not beyond it in time and space, but rather at its incomparable construction. That is the special thing which supplies us with an answer. The whole answer however is only gained if we leave aside all questions as to the time of origin of any species. Such a time does not exist. If it did, we would not be able to ascertain the incomparability and duality of special construction, since temporal things are not eternally discernible, which constructions of incomparable things however are, as experience clearly shows. We cannot prove directly and by pointing to a contradiction inherent to the thing, that no species can have an origin in time. Such a proof pertains to things theoretical and hypothetical. We can prove, however, as we did just above, that experience and knowledge would contradict each other if a species could originate in time. Such a proof proceeds by means of analogy, as it did when it was proven, in our philosophy, that the earth is located at the centre of the universe, and by means of the analogy of experience and knowledge, in our present example, where the experience of the infinite existence of a neutral organization's incomparable construction and at the same time the knowledge of the arbitrary nature of time, rule out the possibility of a special origin in time.

*

Book II

It is our wish to discover exactly how neutral organizations are relate and what it means, that they are totally related, in order to come to a better understanding of varying organizations. We know that a neutral organization is constructed of two incomparable things, that these two incomparables are a structure and a sphere of influence, and that the structures of all neutral organizations are alike while their spheres of influence are one and the same. On top of this we have found out that the construction of incomparables, as in the case of neutral organizations, is a special thing, and that all such constructions which stem from the same order, meaning that each of the two comparable must in every case have the same origin, are called a species.

The structures of all neutral organizations are alike. What this means, in comparison to being the same for instance and to being different, has to do specifically with the general comparability of all phenomena, which we will now discuss.

Phenomenal difference, difference as we experience it and understand it, may lie in any and all possible aspects of comparable things. That is how it differs from apparent difference, which pertains only to the surface of things and can therefore not be judged. We need not concern ourselves with the latter since science deals only with phenomena.

Two things may be comparable and at the same time different from each other in every aspect. They are not comparable however if they are different in no aspect.

For two things to be the same they must at least be comparable, and therefore some difference must exist between them which allows us not only to distinguish between them, which we can also do between incomparable things, but also to discern how it comes that they may be compared and then to ascertain the bond of comparison. This bond may occasion simply a difference. It may also be the root of their being alike, similar, the same or one. Each of these must be treated individually.

Let us first again be in the clear about this: that such a state of being exists where two things may be distinguished one from the other without their being comparable to each other. For the sake of precision we will say that they do not have a common bond, but that they are bonded, or bounded. Such a state of incomparable duality does not exist either in a limited or in an unlimited fashion, but it is in itself a limit and the root of all limitation. It should also be added here that there is no such thing as the limit, since a thing must exist before it can exist in one way or another, which implies that freedom succeeds limitation, and in turn that an absolute state is achieved in a way. Therefore an absolute limit is an impossibility.

For two things to be comparable then, they must not only be distinguishable from each other, but they must possess a distinguishable bond. This bond exists as a third thing and must be understood as such, on its own terms and not only in relation to the things it joins.

The most fundamental bond which can exist between two things and which may join them is a degree of difference. It comes about through condition, situation and state, through all three of these at once, and it may be understood in terms of them.

In terms of the condition or conditions under which comparable things exist, they are fundamentally joined as parts. This implies a degree of difference in size. No two parts of the same thing
can be the same size, and if two things are of the same size they
cannot become joined. The two halves of any single thing for
example are either exactly the same size, in which case they can
not become the thing of which they are halves but must be treated
as potentially whole things rather than as parts; or else they differ to a degree in size, in which case they may be referred to as
conditional halves rather than as exact halves, but what counts is
that they may at an time be joined and become that thing of which
they are the two parts.

In terms of the situation in which comparable things exist,
they are fundamentally joined as units or as increments, one or
the other depending on whether the situation in which they exist is total and whole or else partial. To be joined as units or as
increments implies a degree of difference in form. No two units
and no two increments can have the same form, and if two
things have the same form they cannot be joined as units or as
increments in one and the same thing. Two apples for example
may be units of the same cake, in which case that cake is their
total situation, and they may be increments of the same sauce, in
which case that sauce is their partial situation if no other ingredient except the two apples has gone into the sauce; and both in
case of the cake and in case of the sauce the form of the two
must differ to a degree. If the two apples have the same form,
either in the case of the sauce of in the case of the cake, then
they are not units or increments of the same thing, of the cake or
of the sauce, but instead they are simply in one mixture or in
another.

We do not suggest here that anyone eat his apple sauce unsea-
soned. A little cinnamon makes it especially delicious. The rudimentary form was meant simply for the sake of demonstration.

In terms of the state in which two comparable things may exist they differ as members of the same thing, which implies a difference in shape. Whatever has the same shape must also have the same form and the same size and, by the same token, if two things differ in shape they do not necessarily differ in form or in size, since shape is all-inclusive. For example if two objects have the same shape then they must be existing in different states and therefore they cannot even be compared, not because they are incomparable, which they are not, but because we cannot experience them at the same time. For things to be incomparable we must be able to view them together and at once.

Organization by members of the same thing means then that a difference in shape exists between them on account of which they are linked.

In retrospect we may say that incomparables are joined, that different parts are combined through a common bond, that different units or increments are united or integrated by means of a specific tie, and that members are linked in a way which we have yet to discover.

Where a condition is always simply a condition and where a situation is either total and whole or else partial, a state is either steady, in which case it is either firm or infirm, or else it is abrupt.

Different members in any state are linked. This link is of a different nature than the members, but in substance of course it is the same. This is a peculiar state of affairs. We can understand the reason for it, since shape is all-inclusive and does not allow us therefore to remove ourselves from it for the sake of perception, neither by means of perspective, as we do in the case of size, nor through transition as we do in the case of form when we perceive it 'a priori' or 'a posteriori'. And while we can understand the reason for this, we are not able to predict it in itself. These two facts always go hand in hand. While we receive the gift, we do not try to gain control over the giver. Science can only succeed in taking account of the entirely new, if it perfects

34

itself by surpassing this one limitation, where it has always insisted on predictability before accepting knowledge.

But it is not reality which we wish to predict, but our understanding of it. Reality on its own is perfectly sound and good. When we understand reality as it is and not as we would like it to be or after we have carelessly interfered with it, we worship in it.

*

of the understanding:

That the understanding is predictable cannot be doubted since we have theoretical knowledge and can draw up hypotheses. Such knowledge can only be potentially understood but it is this potential understanding on the basis of which truth again is possible, and if only enough truth comes to light we will soon see a reality which has no flaw and corresponds to our most precious experience of life.

More directly, we are able to predict our understanding and to attain potential knowledge only on the basis of what little knowledge and understanding we are born with. But this is to be remembered and always again to be reminded, that the smallest amount of actual wisdom promises the greatest degree of potential wisdom, and rightly so, since man is to be perfected and not to be overwhelmed. If we only imagine how our minds would react to a direct ratio between power and dimension we soon give up wishing that such a thing were the case.

It is our ability to think however which profits directly from the nature of things as they are. Rational thought accepts this nature and irrational thought resists it. Both kinds of thought are important and valuable. This may at first strike us as a puzzle, since we may have accustomed ourselves either to accepting only rational thought or else perhaps to resisting irrational thought. But if irrational thought is in itself a resistance to the nature of things it makes no sense at all to resist it again, and then the product of those two resistances once more perhaps and so on until we have exhausted our stamina and have grown none the more clever for it. Also, since rational thought accepts the nature of things and since this acceptance of the true nature of all things is its very own nature, why should it not also accept its own brother which is irrational thought, whose true nature as another real thing is the resistance of the nature of things? There can be found no reason why it should not accept its own brother, and in fact it should. No one demands of us that we should judge thought itself whether it is rational or irrational except from time to time our own faulty judgment. It is the products of our thought which require judgment, not their source and origin. Therefore, whenever we incline to approach thought itself for the purpose of judging it we should decline and reproach ourselves, else we are like the diver who forgot to rise to the surface because he became so engrossed in the beauty of the fauna and flora near the sea bed.

In conclusion, if we wish to be champions of rational thought we should turn that thought fully even towards irrational thought, its opposite, and persist in our ambition, which means that we resist nothing which is real. And naturally irrational thought is real, since if it were not we should not be able to think in that fashion. Simply not choosing something does not make it any the less real. If on the other hand we do not prefer one kind of thought over the other but instead strive simply to think, leaving the particular direction and quality of our thought as much to the product of our thought which has chosen us as its master as to the master who shapes and guides it on its way to perfection and fulfilment, then we will never be troubled about thought itself and may rest assured in the pleasure of its activity and in the enjoyment of its fruit. This conclusion is not so much a categorical imperative as a moral plea.

Now whether we choose to think rationally or in simplicity, we must know what thought is to begin with, and it is to this end that we now direct our energies.

*

Thought is the understanding of the mind. Knowledge of the mind is another thing.

In order to understand our mind we must first be free from it. This freedom is achieved through sufficient application of all the senses available to us.

It is the nature of the senses to train themselves. Training in turn is a purposeful union of all available capabilities. Therefore whatever our senses are capable of must be utilized by them for a single purpose if they are ever to be in their own possession. And such is the free mind, that it is in fact one single sense, in the sense that all the senses are united in their attempt to achieve one common goal.

A certain sense is in its own possession when it is fully trained. At such a time it is linked organically to the body and to the soul. Now since the body is in fact nothing else than the total combination of our senses, and since the soul is the combination of these senses as a whole, we conclude that a particular sense is fully trained when it belongs as much to the body as to the soul, and in other words when it is no more at the mercy of one than in the service of the other.

The first step in the training of our senses is concentration. This does not mean that we concentrate them on anything else, but simply that we concentrate them. It is not necessary to look at a think in order to see it, and similarly it is not required that we see a thing if we wish to see. Seeing is an activity like all other activities, free in itself of objective or subjective considerations and concerns, and so it is with all the senses. Even the sense of taste, which is not strictly a sense because it cannot partake in vision, is nevertheless by nature independent of reality and in itself a real thing.

Concentration then has to do only with our senses or, which is to say the same thing, only with our body and our soul, and with nothing inside or outside of these or in any way related to them. When we concentrate, we focus our attention on itself. The immediate outcome of this is primarily increased attention. And there is no limit to this. Our attention snowballs.

When our attention has increased to the point where we have become unaware of all things except that to which we pay attention, it turns into consciousness. Only if we do our utmost, this seems clear, can we pay attention to the degree of consciousness. It must be stressed however that consciousness is not a degree of applied attention. The two cannot be measured along the same scale. Attention must be pushed forward until suddenly we find that we have become conscious.

We know that we are conscious when we have become conscious of what we have never been conscious of before to the best of our knowledge. This is the sign. If we were always conscious, we would never be without a totally new thing to deal with.

Consciousness is not self-sustaining. Sufficient attention must always be paid. It happens that our consciousness grows and that at the same time our attention, instead of continually supporting us consciously, flags. At such a moment irritations and disturbances set in, and perturbations of the mind. They are both physical and mental, and are meant to return us to the road upon which we had initially set out.

There are two ways of dealing with these disturbances. One is physical and the other is mental. We either approach them with our whole being or else only with our mind.

The mental approach to unconscious material requires above all power, whereas the physical approach to unconscious material depends upon nothing else. Our body and soul are able to deal with what disturbs their peace and tranquillity by simple adaptation, without reference to any inner or outer thing. Disorders are immediately fulfilled and lacks of consequence reoriented. The mind participates in this as another one of an infinite number of organs and does nothing on its own. Such a state of being is called simple living.

Complexities set in as soon as the mind begins to work independently. We cannot say, of course, that the mind works independently of the soul and the body, because once it does work independently the body and soul are not any more whole, but disoriented. The independent mind therefore has only one purpose, which is to turn squarely towards the disoriented body and soul and to operate. Operation then is the application of all independent mental energies to the disoriented body and soul for the purpose of establishing an over-all unity.

The disoriented body and soul independently of the mind is the flesh, and it is of no concern to us.

The unity of mind, body and soul, when the mind operates purposefully and with singular intent, which it can only do if it leaves aside all matters excepting the body and the soul in whatever state of disorientation they might presently find themselves – this is not the same as the physical wholeness which exists when the mind is a part of the body. There is no need to speak of body and soul while the mind is a physical thing, but only of body or only of soul, whichever our taste prefers, since in such a case of physical wholeness no difference can exist. So instead of 'physical' one might also say 'spiritual' if one did not care about appropriateness to the times. But since we sacrifice nothing that is true by appealing to popular taste and can only gain by adapting our language, insofar as it is a mode of expression, to the particular needs of the present time in history, we will say physical instead of spiritual and body instead of soul at such times and in such places where the difference between the two has no meaning and in fact does not exist. Of course it would be a grave error if one strove to diminish this difference where and whenever it does exist. It may be our duty and pleasure to keep body and soul together, but never to assimilate them, which is essentially a fortuitous occurrence and exists through the presence of grace.

Aside and on top of physical wholeness, which is holiness, and mental unity, there is also mechanical oneness.

In the case of physical wholeness the mind participates. It partakes of the body and collaborates with it. In the case of mental unity the mind operates and orients. Upon the success of the mind's operation and once orientation has become total and complete, the mind is free. In such a state the mind is a perfectly mechanical being and may be described as a machine. During that time the body (or the soul) is one with the mind and may be described as an automatic being or as an automaton. The body and mind as one in this case are a mechanism.

We have isolated now the three possible kinds of thought. They are simple thought, (which involves complex thought); rational thought, (which involves irrational thought); and pure thought, (which involves all other thought, which is not pure but it does not involve such a thing as impure thought, which cannot be conceived). Even as all thought is an understanding of the mind, so is simple thought an understanding of physical wholeness; so is rational thought an understanding of mental unity and so is pure thought an understanding of mechanical oneness. In each of these three cases the mind which is being understood is, as we have learned, a different being, partaking here of the body, operating upon it there, and then being one with it as a mechanism. (We guard here against metaphysical conceit which commonly expresses itself in extraordinary locution. It would be wrong for example to say that the mind, in the case of pure thought is mechanically one with the body, since oneness excludes and precludes any mechanical activity. We could say that it is mechanistically one with the body, since the two are a mechanism in this case, and since all activity does not cease. But we make do with our statement, that mind and body in the case of pure thought are one as a mechanism, since we see no reason in paying tribute to that again which is meant as a tribute to us. In short, we will try not to describe attributes, but to put them to work.)

There are three kinds of thought, but there is only one kind of action.

Thought and action concur.

The kind of thought which concurs with action causes or influences it to be action of one sort or another.

Action is based on thought. Without thought there can be no action. Similarly does thought depend upon action, and without action there can be no thought. But thought is never based on action, but on the truth, and action never depends upon thought, but only on circumstance. The relationship of action and thought is rational.

Just as the word expresses the universe so does a ratio express the world. This is its purpose. A rational relationship is the result of rational thought, and rational thought results from a confrontation with the world. The world is unique in that it is related to nothing. One might define it picturesquely as the shadow of the word, which word relates all things.

While a confrontation with the world results eventually in a ratio, the confrontation with the word results in a word. The word regenerates itself while the world relates other things. This is the purpose of the world, that all things which come into contact with it become related to each other.

We come now to that most prized of all human abilities, which is the ability to predict.

The one important thing to remember here is that primordially, before any order can exist, there must be either a vision of or-

41

der or else an ordered dream. We have discussed both of these phenomena in our philosophy; vision not very extensively, but as the illumination of all sense perception, which differs from sight even as reason differs from consciousness, and dream, which deals in mere phenomena, such as are not only devoid of matter, but whose appearance is even without recognizable content.

We differentiate now on one hand between visions of parts of the universe, which present us with its detail, and visions of the universe per se; and on the other hand between dreams of members of the world, which give us the world in detail, and dreams of the world in itself.

The understanding is able to deal with all four categories, according to their origin and purpose. We shall take up such dreams first which give us the world as a whole.

Here we must familiarize ourselves with what is referred to in eschatology as the four last things. These are the categories of the distinct imagination insofar as it receives an imprint of the purpose of all creation. This purpose is in reality not phenomenal and can therefore not be scientifically approached and scrutinized. It can be stated in many ways, such as through revelation as the effective glorification of God or poetically as the unselfish love of every man, which is the same; or perhaps prophetically as the preparation for the coming of the light, and philosophically in terms of a theodicy or on the basis of creative love itself. Science however allows us to understand things, and so it comes that we turn to or experience of them which in the present case is the mere appearance of the world, but of the whole world, and in a four-fold pattern due to the workings of the imagination which must be understood properly and in singular fashion.

The four divisions which will be collated are willpower, truth, justice and want. They are all reflections of one another and have nothing common except this their source. For that reason we must deal with them as reflections only, and not as reflections of some other quantity outside of them, or even as things in themselves, which they decidedly are not at this moment.

Willpower lends itself to analysis. The doctrine of the will as an all-comprehensive force or as a drive is of no help to us here since thought, which springs from the will, is free. Power of the will is therefore not an organic faculty, something which one can use, but a possession, after which one strives and in the enjoyment of which one rests. Consequently the link between this willpower and its reflection as truth is by way of memory. Truth as it appears here cannot be understood directly but only through the transmission of time. In other words it does not lie in our power to achieve clarity immediately, but we must condescend to the duration of the event which we have become part of, and we must leave the ultimate extent of this duration in other hands than ours. What we can do to the fullness of our strength is to rely upon our knowledge of every event's certain completion, and furthermore, if we wish, although this is not necessary, we may rest assured in our faith as masters of the universe and of all creation.

Once a truth of this nature has been comprehended, which may be likened to the digestion and assimilation of a fine nourishment, it becomes more apparent, when we judge from within the added knowledge gained in this way, that it is justice alone on the basis of which the world can endure. Were it able to continue upon a foundation of the truth, there would be no need of a world, since all things, including the understanding, which would then always be our understanding and perfect, would be primordially related, or, since this is an absurdity in metaphor, all would be well. But since all is not well, and since therefore a world must exist as a result of which all things, including our understanding, may be consequently related, this world must be ruled in justice and governed and administered according to justice, and not in terms of the truth. Attempts to do the latter are pipedreams and stem from an inconsequent utility of illusion.

All things pertaining to justice and alone to justice can be summed up under the law. But the law itself cannot be understood; only manifestations of it. It is possible however to divine the origin of the law, which is a gift, and it is important to keep both of these facts firmly in mind. No one is able to captivate the original and principal mainspring of the law which sets off the individual mechanisms of the law's manifestations. This is not available to man. To some however it is given to interpret the distinct manifestations of the law as they occur in time and to ponder them so as to discover how they are rooted meaningfully in the universal course of events. Such persons are then able to predict these special events and to adapt them to the world, so that the world may profit from them.

Want is the reason of all that belongs to the world and stems from it. This must be understood in the light of the world as an unrelated thing. It endures in isolation: which must strike us as a paradox, indeed as the primeval paradox itself, until we admit that this endurance is a persistence with a definite and particular end in view. This end is always unreal and never real. It serves in that way so that the world may remain in isolation.

Want is longing and desire for things which are unnecessary and not good. (It is possible even to want bad things, but we need not go into that at present.) Whatever is neither good nor bad is indifferent, and it is such things which we want when we are part of the world.

Indifferent things are not things which are the same. In order to be the same, an understandable relationship must exist. In order to be indifferent, no relationship may exist. Prior to the existence of the world therefore nothing was either related or unrelated, but all things were simply what they were. Such a state may be referred to as chaos, and it can never come about again. Nevertheless we recall that once it existed. Our reason for doing this is twofold. On one hand, if we wish to understand the world as it is, in other words realistically, we must avail ourselves of its reason for coming into being. On the other hand, if we wish to live in the world, as we all eventually must whether we wish to or not, we do well to acquaint ourselves thoroughly with the world's actual characteristics, and this may prove difficult, since culture and civilization, which are organized resistance to the world and the acceptance of the world through its recreation, do not always match a well as it would seem or as easily as one would prefer. Consequently one suffers. An understanding of the world however as a natural by-product of order in the face of chaos, and a study of its behaviour as such a by-product in the reflected light of its isolated position in the universe and as a being which always wants but never knows what it wants allows us to live in it, without suffering at best and in mere coexistence with it at worst when all our powers of resistance and receptivity have become depleted, as they must now and then if we are to become perfect, until such a time as due to recreation and relation by means of culture and civilization nothing remains of the world but its outer garment of dominion which is then simply turned inside out and becomes the bridal gown of our salvation.

*

For what I wish to say now I find the German language more suitable.

*

Die Voraussage gelingt uns, sobald wir uns von ihren Grundlagen genügend überzeugt haben.

Man unterscheide zwischen Voraussage und Vorhersage. Diese stützt sich auf Erfahrenes, jene auf Erlebtes.

Das Erlebnis versteht sich von selbst. Es genügt, einzelne Erlebnisse ganz aufzufassen, um sich ihre Substanz anzueignen. (Wen das erschrickt, der Befindet sich schon auf dem richtigen

45

Weg.) Die Erfahrung jedoch will zuerst verstanden sein. Man kann also erleben ohne sich dessen unbeding bewusst zu sein, wenn man nur seiner Sache, das heißt des Erlebnisses, sicher ist. Erfahrung jedoch verlangt vollen Einsatz des Bewusst- seins und diesen Einsatz sozusagen im Namen des Verstandes.

Auf dieser Einsicht in den Unterschied zwischen Erfahrung und Erlebnis beruht die erste Tatsache in Bezug auf Voraussage und Vorhersage. Das ist die Übelkeit (Nausea).

Wie immer bezieht sich die Wissenschaft auch hier auf allgemein Menschliches. Gerade dadurch verliert man sich im Unnützen wenn man meint das Wissenswerte beschäme. Als Grund aller Wissenschaft leuchtet jedoch des einzelnen Menschen Wohl und Weh am triftigsten ein.

Die Übelkeit, so wie wir sie hier erkennen wollen, bezeichnet einen Zustand des Menschenlebens. Man kann sich also nicht darüber hinweg setzen. Was uns interessiert ist jedoch nicht dieser Zustand selbst, sondern inwiefern er Voraussetzung ist und Erkenntnisgrund letzten Endes für das Voraussagen und das Vorhersagen.

Durch diese beiden Tätigkeiten setzen wir uns mit Zukünftigem in Verbindung. Im Falle des Voraussagens benutzen wir bewusst den Verstand. Im Falle des Vorhersagens jedoch halten wir uns an die Vernunft. Welche von beiden Tätigkeiten wir wählen hängt nicht von uns ab. Eine von beiden jedoch müssen wir wählen, denn beide zugleich lassen sich nicht unternehmen. Wo Entschluss und Entscheidung keine Rolle spielen dürfen, wo jedoch eine Wahl getroffen werden soll wenn wir unserem persönlichen Wachstum nicht aus dem Wege gehen wollen, da müssen wir uns dann ganz den Umständen überlassen. Was wir dadurch aufgeben ist nicht unser Wille, da es uns jederzeit frei steht uns dem Imperativ der Umstände wieder zu entziehen, sondern unseren Intellekt. Merkmale einer solchen Hingabe des denkenden Individuums sind das Vertrauen auf die Wirklichkeit als ein Ganzes und der Glaube an die Möglichkeit des universalen Wissens. Beide Merkmale sind Einstellungen des Gemüts und lassen sich deshalb nicht vom bestimmenden Gewissen trennen. Man erkennt also hier inwiefern diese Hingabe des denkenden Intellekts keine bloße Pose sein darf wenn man das Urteil erreichen will wodurch entweder die Voraussage oder die Vorhersage, eine jedoch von beiden, möglich wird. Man verlässt sich auf jene Realität, welche unter allen Umständen der Fall ist, mögliche eingeschlossen, und kann sich deshalb keines unterscheidenden Tuns und Lassens bewusst bleiben. Solange solches noch vorhanden ist, hat man den Prozess der handelnden Passivität noch nicht vollzogen, und umgekehrt lässt sich die Vollständigkeit dieses Vollzugs an der Reinheit der oben erwähnten Gemütseinstellungen feststellen, und nicht etwa auf irgendwelche Weise durch, oder am, Intellekt, wie das schließlich sogar klar vorstellbar ist.

Infolgedessen leidet man und tut es zweckmäßig.

Ein bestimmter Zweck kann unmöglich diesem Leiden vorausgesetzt werden, denn dafür benötigte man den Intellekt, der uns im Moment nicht gehört. Zwecklos kann dieses Leiden jedoch auch nicht sein, denn wir wissen was wir tun und wissen zugleich warum wir es tun. Die Zweckmäßigkeit dieses Leidens ist also unbestimmt und allgemein, welches bedeutet, daß sir für alle möglichen Eindrücke offen und aufnahmebereit sind, und daß wir uns zugleich keinem wirklichen Eindruck entziehen. Wir sagen bewusst Eindrücke und nicht Sinneseindrücke, da wir weder den Schmerz noch den entferntesten Zufall ausschließen.

Hat man die Gemütsverfassung erreicht welche aus einem bewussten Vertrauen und aus einem bestimmten Glauben besteht, und will man sich weiterhin damit einlassen, so kommt es auf zweierlei an: erstens auf unsere Haltung den Eindrücken gegenüber, welche eintreffen oder nicht; und zweitens auf die Verarbeitung dieser Eindrücke, welche unternommen wird oder nicht, und in jenem Falle zu einem Grad oder ganz durchgeführt wird.

Hier kommt es nun darauf an ob wir richtig falsch voraus- und vorhersagen. Es besteht wohl immer das Verlangen, den Eindrücken, welche uns noch unbekannt sind, zuvorzukommen. Jeder neue Eindruck bringt dieses Verlangen als Kapazität mit sich und löst es in uns aus. Wir sollen uns dem Unbekannten bloßstellen und alles hinnehmen was uns gereicht wird. Gleich gehen uns schlimme Ahnungen auf. Je schmerz-licher unsere Erfahrung und je enttäuschender unsere Erlebnisse bis hierher gewesen, desto schwerer fällt es uns natürlich, der gänzlich neuen Wirklichkeit gegenüberzutreten. Zwei Fehler sind also zu vermeiden, welche den Erfolg unseres Vorhabens kompromittieren. Bloß der Wirklichkeit gegenübertreten bedeutet nicht ihre Annahme. Wir sollen uns diese beiden Tatsachen nicht umgekehrt vorstellen sondern in wahrer und wirkungsgemäßer Reihenfolge. Die Ersatzwirklichkeit, die unseren autonomen Reaktionen entspringt, geschieht immer in falscher Reihenfolge, also rückwärts. Man stellt sich die Gefahr so groß vor wie sie das schlechte Gewissen ausmalt, statt sie so auszumalen wie sie das Wissen uns vorstellt. Dann kommt es auf unser Gewissen selbst an. Einerseits stellt es uns das Gesetz dar, welches wir weder übertreten wollen noch können. Ob wir ihm jedoch folgen, darauf kommt es an. Um dem Gesetz zu folgen und um seine Pflicht zu erfüllen, dazu gebraucht es den Intellekt. Hier scheidet sich nun die große Masse der Menschen. Viele erschrek- ken schon vor den ersten Anzeichen des Gesetzes und handeln sofort ihnen gemäß. Das erleichtert die Spannung dem Unbe- kannten gegenüber und das folgliche Gefühl des Wohlgefallens wird in Selbsthochachtung übersetzt. Andere halten momentan aus und schauen sich dieses Gesetz an, welches ihnen in ihrem Gewissen entgegentritt. Denn andererseits enthält unser Gewis- sen nicht nur das Gesesztz in all seinen Punkten und Feinheiten, sondern es besteht auch aus den Erklärungen, Berechnungen und Anwendungsmöglichkeiten dieses Gesetzes. Jede Erfahrung und jedes Erlebnis spiegelt sich also in besonderer Weise auf un-

serem Gewissen, und es bedarf nur unserer einführenden Zustim-
mung und schon überreicht uns der Verstand ein passendes Pro
und Kontra, demgemäß wir den gegenwärtigen Fall regeln. So
geschieht es, sollten wir betonen, solange wir über unseren Intellekt verfügen und sobald wir ihn wieder in unsere Gewalt bringen.
Verharren wir jedoch weiterhin in unserem Vorhaben als bewusst
Leidende, so lehnen wir diese Verstandeslösung unserer durch
das Fremde hervorgerufene Spannung ab und blicken genauer
auf unser Gewissen. Da wirkte nun die bestimmte Erfahrung
oder das besondere Erlebnis wie ein Schlüssel, der uns nicht
nur das zutreffende Gesetz, dem Einzelfall unterliegend, sondern
das Gesetz überhaupt zeigt, und uns nicht nur etliche Regeln in
die Hände legt, die wir auf die Erfahrung anwenden, sondern
auf den einzigen Weg weist, auf dem sich jegliches Gesetz ver-
wirklicht.

Jedoch diesen Weg sehen heißt noch nicht ihn betreten. Hier
kehren nun viele um, denn es ist ihnen nicht gegeben ihr gänz-
liches Wollen dieser einzigen Maßnahme und alles einschließ-
enden Regel unterzuordnen. Sie zucken zusammen und wenden
sich ab. Das Gedächtnis erfährt einen kleinen Stich, von dem es
sich bald wieder erholt, und dieser Mensch wird sich in Zukunft
nicht ganz so weit in die Fremde vorwagen.

Wieder andere Menschen bleiben vor diesem einzigartigen
Geschehnis ihres offenbarten Gewissens stehen und besinnen
sich. Wie, fragen sie sich, wenn ..? Nun geschieht in dieser Besinnung so manches. Man steht sozusagen mit dem Rücken der
wildfremden Realität zugekehrt und beschaut sich sein Inneres.
Überrascht entdeckt man hier nun dieselbe Wirklichkeit deren
besonderen Auswirkung man eben erst freien Lauf gelassen, und
findet darüber hinaus noch ein Neues, welches, obwohl total unbekannt, zugleich auch allem Anschein nach, sich mit uns ver-
binden will. Wir erwarten nicht mehr in unbestimmter Ge-müts-
verfassung den unbekannten Eindruck indem wir unsere Sinne
ausnahmslos dazu benutzen diese Gemütsverfassung rein zu

erhalten, sondern wir benutzen unsere Sinne um das Unbekannte zu begreifen, welches anhand unseres Gewissens wahr und in Wirklichkeit plötzlich vor uns auftauchte.

Alles wissenschaftlich Erkennbare, die Welt der Phänomene also, ist zweidimensional. Einerseits handelt es sich um Mesurabilien, also um solches das gemessen ist und gemessen werden kann; und andererseits um Taten und Prozesse, die sich nicht messen lassen, denen aber ein Maß innewohnt. Beide Dimensionen sind zugleich erfahrbar und erlebbar.

Diese Teilung in zwei Dimensionen ist allgemein menschlich. Das Höchste und Tiefste dessen sich ein Mensch bewusst werden kann hängt von dieser Zweiteilung ab, denn sie schließt sich selbst in ihren Prozess mit ein. Eine Dimension allein lässt sich nicht vorstellen. Mehr als zwei Dimensionen setzen notwendig einen Vergleichswert voraus der sich nie ganz diesseitig aufheben lässt. Einen transzendentalen Überrest muss man ihnen wohl oder übel immer zugeben. Nur im Falle von zwei Dimensionen, der schon im Wort selbst liegt (ich meine hier nicht unbedingt das Wort Dimension obwohl ich es nicht ausschließen möchte) lässt sich eine Teilung des wissenschaftlich Realen durchführen, in der selbst alles Wissenswerte ans Licht kommt und durch welche allein man dem Verstand ohne jeglichen Vorbehalt gerecht wird. Natürlich wird dieser Verstand sich dann auch selbstständig zu behaupten wissen.

In der Teilung liegt, und durch die Teilung erscheint, alles Wissenswerte, und nicht auf Grund dieser Teilung oder als ihre etwaige Konsequenz. Deshalb lassen sich auch beide Hälften des Gezweiteilten zugleich und auf einmal betrachten, weil sonst keine Substanz nötig ist durch die man erst die Teilung unternehmen kann, welche Substanz dann freilich im erwünschten und erstrebten Gesamtbild fehlen muss.

Kehren wir zurück zu unserem Gewissen, so erkennen wir auch hier die Möglichkeit aus dem Gesetz und seinen Anwendungen die gesamte wissenschaftlich erkennbare Wirklichkeit dadurch abzuleiten, indem wir das Gewissen auf dieselbe zweidimensionale Weise spalten. Diese Einsicht erreichen wir sobald wir der Besinnung gemäß, also durch selbstbezogene und gesammelte Anwendung aller unserer vorhandenen Sinne, unser Gewissen auf seinen stofflichen Inhalt hin überprüfen.

Gerade die Anwesenheit eines stofflichen Inhalts überhaupt im Gewissen gibt uns zu tun. Die Neugier allein fordert uns heraus nachzufragen, was eigentlich durch ein ganz reines Gewissen zu erreichen sei. Besteht das Gesetz noch, ohne die Notwendigkeit seiner möglichen Anwendung? Die Frage berührt das Sakrale des Gesetzes – rührt es jedoch keineswegs an. Gesetzt – so spekuliert der Unternehmungslustige – das Gesetz überhaupt, käme erst dadurch instand, daß ein Stoff, und sogleich natürlich auch der notwendig dazugehörige Träger, sich als Widerstand aufwirft? Man weiß noch von keinem Gegenstand für diesen Widerstand, aber trotzdem ist es uns erlaubt die Einheit von Gesetz und Stoff als trägen Widerstand theoretisch festzusetzen.

Und so erkennen wir auch bald, als Resultat dieser Theorie, die rein gewissenhafte, stoff- und trägerlose, und von allem Gesetz befreite Gegenwart der wirklichen Substanz. Als besonderer Gegenstand erscheint sie uns in der Gestalt des freien Willens. Was diesem Willen widerstrebt, aus egal welchem Grunde und egal zu welchem Zweck, unterwirft sich ihm mechanisch, und so entsteht das Gesetz, welches sich dem freien Willen anpasst statt in ihm aufzugehen, und der Stoff, der, von der jeweiligen zeitlichen Erscheinung des Gesetzes getragen, den freien Willen wiedergibt und wiederholt.

Alles Gesetzliche, einschließlich jedes Gesetz und das Gesetz überhaupt, besteht also gegenüber dem freien Willen und immer nur anhand des reinen Gewissens, welcher Wille und welches Gewissen zusammen das sind, was wir Substanz nennen.

Diese Substanz ist es nun wieder, auf die sich alles Vorhersagen und Voraussagen stützt insofern es nicht nur Endliches erzielt. Natürlich gehören alle Ziele und Zwecke der bloßen Erscheinung auch zur Wirklichkeit, aber diese allein, unabhängig von Gutem und Richtigem, lassen sich nicht vorausbestim-men, denn sie sind schließlich entweder Symptome oder Kategorien. Was also nicht substantiell ist lässt sich nicht an der Zukunft ablesen.

Nun setzt sich unser Verstand auf zweierlei Art und Weise mit aller wirklichen Substanz in Verbindung: einmal durch die Reflexion, und dann auch durch Weissagung und Wahrsag-ung. Auf letztere deuteten wir in unserer Philosophie als ‚intuitive' Kontemplation. Das Wort *künden* beschreibt beide.

Reflexion ist Anwendung der Sinne auf die Substanz. Künden ist Anwendung der Substanz auf die Sinne. In beiden Fällen handelt es sich um einen Weg, auf dem ein bestimmtes Resultat erreicht wird. Die Bedeutung des Resultats kommt ganz auf denVerstand an.

Der Verstand deutet auf dem Weg der Reflexion und auf dem des Kündens.

Unser ganzes Vermögen die Zukunft vorauszubestimmen hängt ab von diesem Vermögen des Verstandes, zu deuten. Was man versteht kann auf zweierlei Weise behandelt werden. Entweder man benutzt es oder man lässt sich davon einschränken und lernt etwas Neues. Will der Verstand deuten, so muss er sich auf letztere Art und Weise absolut kategorisch entweder durch die Besinnung, reflexionsgemäß, oder anhand des gewissen Glaubens, substanzgemäß, bestimmen lassen. Innerhalb dieser Grenzen bewegt er sich frei, da er sie sich selbst auferlegt hat. Durch diese absolut kategorische Immanenz alles Verstehens wird die Zeit nur vonseiten ihrer chronologischen Simultaneität her betrachtet, und alles Nacheinander, abgebrochen oder ewig, wird abseits und außer Auge liegen gelassen.

Das Simultane der Uhrzeit – man dürfte es auch Urzeit nennen – wirkt nervend. Das psychosomatische System allein wird angeregt und zu seinem völligen Ausmaß. Die Dauer dieser Wirkung, also daß sie dauert und solange sie dauert, bestimmt das Vermögen des Verstandes zu deuten. Alle Tätigkeit der Einbildungskraft wird nun nicht wie sonst verstandesgemäß angewendet, sondern auf immanenten Gehalt hin oder als Ding an sich untersucht. Sollte reine Wirklichkeit und Inhalt zusammentreffen, wie das oben im Falle unseres Gewissens geschah, so wende man sich anfänglich dem Inhalt zu und dann erst dem Substanziellen.

Nehmen wir diesen komplizierteren Fall an. Der Inhalt, das Stoffliche also, zusammen mit der besonderen Darbringung des Stoffes, wird zuallererst abgesondert. Es dreht sich hier nicht um Abstraktion, sondern um ihr diametral-polares Gegenstück, die Erfindung. Deshalb können wir auch nicht vonGehalt sprechen, weil dieser uns den Stoff dem Gesetz gemäß vorstellt, was uns im Moment gar nichts angeht. Man nehme zum Beispiel einen Hund, der im Sand spielt. Der Inhalt, daß ein Hund hier im Sand spielt, und der Träger dieses Stoffes, nämlich daß hier im Sand gespielt wird, diese werden nur bemerkt und dann beiseite geschoben. (Natürlich müssen sie erst bemerkt werden, sonst könnten wir uns nicht absichtlich von ihnen wegwenden.) Was bleibt ist nichts mehr und nichts weniger als die Wirkung dieses trägen Stoffes auf unser Gemüt, welche wir automatisch durch Ausdruck bezeichnen. Die reale Gegenwart dieses Ausdrucks wird also durch die Wirkung des trägen Stoffs ermöglicht, und diese Wirkung wiederum geschieht deshalb, weil der im Sand spielende Hund rein als Stoff aufgefasst wurde. Wie die Erscheinung des Ausdrucks aussieht hat nichts mit diesem Stoff zu tun. Sie widerspiegelt ihn nicht, deutet nicht auf ihn, erklärt ihn oder umgekehrt betrachtet ihn nicht, und so fort; denn nur ihre Existenz, ihr Dasein verdankt sie dem wirkenden Stoff, und nicht etwa ihr Wesen, welches schicklich und gefügt ist. Das Verhältnis zwischen rein stofflich aufgefasstem Eindruck und dem resultierenden Ausdruck is rein sachlich.

Dreht es sich nun jedoch nicht direkt um den Eindruck der Wirklichkeit sondern um diese Wirklichkeit selbst, so interessiert uns nicht mehr der Fall, sondern alles Andere in Bezug auf diesen Fall und ihm als Einzelfall untergeordnet. Vertrauen wir uns wieder dem Beispiel des Hundes, der im Sand spielt. Daß es ein Hund ist, der hier im Sand spielt, und daß hier im Sand gespielt wird, das sondern wir ab und lassen es rein stofflich auf uns wirken. Nun halten wir jedoch mit dem Ausdruck zurück. Die Wirkung des trägen Stoffes resultiert also nicht, sondern sie setzt sich in Beziehung mit der Substanz unseres Willens und unseres Gewissens. Nun geschieht etwas: Die gesamte Gegenwart unseres geschichtlichen Daseins muss auf einen einzigen Nenner zusammen kommen, welcher Tatsache heißt. Es muss so geschehen, weil die rein erkannte Wirkung des Stofflichen substantiell ist; weil die Substanz, auf welche diese Wirkung trifft, unversal ist; und weil Dasein und Existenz eben gerade dieses bedeuten: ein Zusammenwirken des Universalen mit dem Besonderen. Die Tatsache, welche nicht resultiert, weder kausal noch zufällig, sondern frei geschieht – und hierher gehört unsere Aufmerksamkeit – ist nicht eine mögliche neben mehreren wirklichen Tatsachen, noch ist sie eine wirkliche unter anderen wirklichen Tatsachen, denn sie ist die einzigartige und unwiederholbare Tatsache selbst. An ihr lässt sich alles Zukünftige ablesen dadurch daß wir sie unumwunden verstehen, nicht auf diese oder jene Eigenschaft hin, oder unter diesen oder jenen Umständen. Auch das Messgerät muss also dem Verstand unterworfen werden, welcher sich selbst der transzendierenden, überdauernden Zeit unterwirft.

Eine Tatsache ist unabhängig von der Zeit. Wie wir uns auch wenden oder stellen, es ist uns nie möglich eine Tatsache auf die Zeit hin oder irgendwie im Zusammenhang mit der Zeit zu beurteilen. Was sich von einer Tatsache wissen lässt bezieht sich auf ihre Erscheinung und auf ihren Gehalt. Die Erscheinung wird betrachtet und unterschieden, in Betreffendes und Zutreffendes, und der Gehalt wird entschieden, entschlossen und endlich erschlossen. Die voraus zu bestimmende Zukunft ergibt sich als Endprodukt beider Vorgänge.

Nehmen wir uns das Beispiel eines vollgeladenen Heuwagens. Die Erscheinung dieses Dings bringt uns die Tatsache vor Augen. Sie lässt sich nun beschreiben unter allen Umständen die uns einfallen, und deren Zahl ist unendlich. Einzig das Licht haben wir nötig. Schon die Farbe lässt sich vom Licht abstrahieren. Der Wagen ist rot, das Heu ist grün. Genausogut könnte der Wagen gelb sein und das Heu blau. Blaues Heu ist gar nicht widernatürlich, denn man hat es vielleicht gefärbt. Aber tatsächlich ist dieser Wagen nun einmal rot und das Heu darauf ist grün, und um diese Erscheinung kommen wir nicht herum.

Die Gestalt, die Form und die Größe des Heuwagens gehen uns nichts an im Moment, denn sie gehören nicht zur Erscheinung sondern zur Wirklichkeit, welche wie oben bewiesen frei von der Escheinung besteht.

Außer den farbigen Umständen des Lichtes fallen uns nun vielleicht andere Transportgelegenheiten ein. Gleich erscheint der Wagen als vierrädriges Holzding mit Deichsel und Eisenbeschlag, und das Heu erscheint uns schwer, lose und kurzgehackt. Es könnte auch leicht, fest und langstielig sein, aber diese Möglichkeit und tausend andere wie sie muss uns gar nicht einfallen um den Heuwagen und das Heu so zu sehen wie sie sind. Dann fällt uns vielleicht die Jahreszeit als Umstand ein, und da es in Wirklichkeit Winter ist, steht dieser Wagen mit seiner Ladung Futter ziemlich verlassen und vergessen auf seinem Platz. Mit der Jahreszeit kam uns nämlich der wahrscheinliche Zweck des Heus in den Sinn, und schon erscheint es als Futter und als hätte man vergessen es in den Schober zu packen. Möglicherweise lies man es stehen um den Krähen Unterschlupf zu bieten. Das ändert jedoch nichts and der Erscheinung der Tatsache, welche nicht wahr ist, sondern wahrscheinlich. Als Nächstes fällt uns die Lust ein mit der wir einmal Kühe und Pferde solches Heu hinunterkauen sahen. Jenes Heu sah heller aus, gelblicher grün, und gleich scheint uns diese Ladung möglicherweise von anderer Sorte oder Qualität. Wir suchen in unserem Gedächtnis, soweit es sich schon mit Erscheinungen befasst hat, nach verwendbaren Kategorien und nach verwandtem Wissen, das aus ähnlichen Tatsachenerscheinungen besteht, und kommen endlich zur Annahme eines kleereichen, feuchten Heus, welches wir unter diesen Umständen und aus wer weiß wieviel Gründen nie kaufen würden. Und so betrachten wir die Erscheinung des beladenen Heuwagens immer näher und weiter, bis wir dessen müde werden oder einfach etwas anderes tun wollen. Zu verwendbarem und nützlichem Stoff gelangen wir auf diese Weise nicht. Wo die Erscheinung herkommt und was hinter ihr steckt, was sie in Wirklichkeit bedeutet und wo es mit ihr hinauswill, da können wir unsere Lebzeiten dran herumraten, und diese Lösung des Rätsels ist so richtig wie jene, wenn sie uns nur gefällt und auch Freude bereitet, denn darauf kommt es bei aller Erscheinung an, und allem Anschein nach wird sich das nie ändern lassen; was wir ja auch nicht hoffen. Ich behaupte einen Sachverhalt zwischen dem Eindruck des oben erwähnten Hundes, der im Sand spielte, und dem Ausdruck des beladenen Heuwagens. Jener erzeugte diesen, sage ich, und wer mir das in Gottes Namen glaubt, der wird dadurch um ein hübsches Erlebnis reicher. Beweisen kann ich den Sachverhalt jedoch nicht, und alle Versuche gekonntes Tun durch geheucheltes Wissen zu ersetzen müssen scheitern.

Die Tatsache, deren Erscheinung oben beschrieben wurde, hat auch Gehalt. Wollen wir uns dieses Gehalts vergewissern, so kommt es uns nicht auf ihre Vorstellung an, sondern auf die Bedeutung des Erlebnisses, welches uns die Tatsache ermöglicht.

Die Erscheinung erfahren wir: der Gehalt jedoch will erlebt sein.

Der Gehalt einer Tatsache ist nicht unabhängig von ihrer Erscheinung. Wie wir uns der Erscheinung gegenüber stellen, so erleben wir auch den Gehalt. Die Erscheinung wird hier nicht betrachtet sondern wir setzen uns ihr aus und lassen sie unumständlich auf uns wirken. Demgemäß ist sie nicht Beschaffenheit und Bedingung, sondern Stoff.

Die Reinheit des Stoffes hängt natürlich von uns ab. Der reinste Stoff liefert den vitalsten Gehalt. Reiner Stoff ist gleich Gehalt, und Gehalt an sich ist nicht zu unterscheiden von Leben.

Die Reinheit des Stoffes, der passiv behandelten Erscheinung, hängt ab mehr spezifisch von der Technik unserer Sinne, also unseres Körpers. Der vollkommene Einsatz unserer gesamten Sinne heißt Leib.

Demgegenüber nennt man den totalen Gehalt einer Tatsache Wirklichkeit oder Realität.

Das Maß eines Erlebnisses ist also unser wirklicher Leib. Nehmen wir uns wieder den gefüllten Heuwagen als Beispiel einer Tatsache. Alles was einige Seiten zurück als Erscheinung beschrieben und durch Beobachtung vorgestellt wurde, lassen wir nun so auf uns wirken als sei die Substanz dieser erscheinenden Tatsache auch unsere eigene. Daß es so ist wissen wir, und warum oder wieso es so ist, das verstehen wir. Beides zusammen bedeutet die Kraft unseres Glaubens. Es fehlt nun nur noch die Ausübung unseres Überzeugtseins. Hier kommt es auf unseren Leib an. Die Erscheinung einer Tatsache ist unendlich, wie wir oben zeigten. Unser Aufnahmevermögen ist jedoch nicht unendlich, sondern begrenzt durch die Notwendigkeit und Güte des lebendigen Moments. Das ständige Wachstum unseres Leibes seiner endlichen Erfüllung entgegen benutzt und verarbeitet immer so viel Stoff wie unsere Sinne verlangen, und dieses Verlangen bleibt immer im Grunde mengenmäßig. Verschiedene Werte, wie das in unserer Philosophie deutlich wurde, erzielen die reine Quantität, die ganz angleichbar ist. Also wird dann der Stoff der Erscheinung den wirkenden Sinnen gemäß uns einverleibt.

Wir können unmöglich wissen wie die Erscheinung auf uns wirkt und auf welchem Wege sich unser Leib ihren Stoff assimiliert. Nur daß es geschieht, dessen können wir uns vergewissern. Jeder Versuch der Fleischwerdung auf die Schliche zu kommen, resultiert in einer Verstümmelung des Leibes. Was von uns abhängt ist die Haltung dem erscheinenden Stoff gegenüber, und dieser Haltung wichtigste Prämisse ist der richtige Begriff der Zeit.

Was im Falle eines Erlebnisses geschieht ist also einmalig, und nur durch sein pures Dasein zu begreifen. Von diesem Dasein auf andere Erlebnisse zu schließen ist Betrug und verdorbene Existenz. Statt sich das Konkrete vom noch nicht ganz Verstandenen zu abstrahieren, schiebt man diese Tat einstweilen hinaus und versucht statt dessen sich die Methode aller Methoden anzueignen, um dann später einmal, wenn man abseits von aller Realität vielleicht Lust dazu verspürte, in aller Heimlichkeit und auf eigene Faust . . . böswillig lässt sich jedoch glücklicherweise nichts zuende denken.

Tatsäschlich war unser Heuwagen rot und das Heu darauf grün. Dieses Rot und Grün interessiert uns also zuerst, aber nicht um es zu betrachten, sondern um es uns allmählich anzueignen, als ewig dauerhaftes Besitztum. Unsere Sinne werden nicht auf die Farben angewandt, sondern auf sich selbst, im Namen der Farben. Das Dasein der Farben ist uns gewiss. Ihr Name verbürgt sie uns. Anhand ihrer Namen werden wir uns der Farben bewusst. Alle Vorstellung dabei ist Geschenk und ohne Weiteres verwertbar. Wer sich Gedanken macht über diese Verwendbarkeit und das vorgestellt Gegebene nicht einfach annimmt, als Erfolg seines Wirkens, der erschwert sich sein Los unnötig. Wer die Vorstellung gar in sein Wirken mit einbezieht, der verwirkt sich sein Glück.

Das Bewusstsein des Rot genügt um die Sinne zu speisen. Seinen Stoff bezeichnen wir als Rötel wie im Falle des Gelben in unserer Philosophie den Ocker: es gibt diesen Rötel, sowie alle Pigmente, natürlich nur in der Wirklichkeit, und nie in ihrer besonderen Vorstellung wo wir den Träger vom Getragenen nicht unterscheiden. Solange man es sich noch nicht abgewöhnt hat Geschichte und Natur auf verschiedenen Substanzen ruhen zu lasse, wird das nicht einleuchten.

Das Grün wird uns bewusst als Pigmenten- oder Farbstoffmischung. Diese Mischung wird als solche verwertet, und nicht erst etwa in Bestandteile zerlegt, was auch schließlich nur in der Vorstellung möglich ist. So wie das Rot hat auch das Grün seine eigentümliche Anwendung und seinen seltenen Gebrauch. Es fördert im Körper alle Verbindungen. Das Rot hingegen erleichtert die Lösung. Die größte Menge von Rot befindet sich daher in der Flüssigkeit des Blutes, wo Sauerstoff, als Inhalt des Geruchsinnes, von seinem Träger in der Luft getrennt und mit dem Körper vereint wird. Das Grün kommt vor im Auge, wo es bei der Verbindung des weißen Lichtes mithilft, und in der Galle, wo die Synthese von Wirkstoffen geschieht.

Die wichtigste Erkenntnis unserer Untersuchung des wissenschaftlichen Vorausbestimmens bezieht sich auf die Phantasie.

Die Phantasie verkörpert zugleich das Tun und das Sein. Beides, Tun und Sein, sind als Phantasie unzertrennbar dargestellt. Wollte man also Gewisses über die Phantasie aussagen, so müsste man sie selbst sprechen lassen, denn außer dieser ihrer einzigartigen Tätigkeitsweise existiert sie nicht.

Nur der Mensch hat Phantasie. Sie entspringt nicht dem Hirn, sondern dem Leib überhaupt. Ihr Dasein ist die Gestaltung. Was Gestalt hat wurde zum Teil oder ganz von der Phantasie her bestimmt. Im Wesen der Gestalt liegt die Vereinbarung von Dasein und Tätigkeit, so wie die Phantasie das ermöglicht.

Die Phantasie, als Produkt des freien Willens, ist gesetzlos. Alles Gesetzliche ist eine Widergabe der lebendigen Phantasie. Sie überliefert das Wachstum. Das Gesetz jedoch begrenzt das Wachstum soweit diese Begrenzung nötig ist um dem wachsenden Ding Gültigkeit zu verleihen. Als Gültigkeit bezeichnen wir die Bedingungen des Werts.

Die Gültigkeit eines Dings ist keineswegs vom Gesetz her bestimmt. Andererseits ist sie jedoch auch keine unausbleibliche Folge der gestaltenden Phantasie. Aber sie ist möglich ganz unabhängig und unbegrenzt vom Gesetz, als Gestaltung der reinen Phantasie, welche sich weder auf das Gesetz stützt, noch ihm widerstrebt, und deshalb das Gesetz erfüllt. Was einst der Freiheit und dem freien Willen widerstrebte und dadurch zum gesetzlichen Stoff wurde, lässt sich von der Phantasie neu gestalten und möglicherweise von der reinen Phantasie ganz umgestalten, um als freies Ding in der sich ereignenden Wirklichkeit dazustehen.

*

I continue in English:

The prediction of the future in terms of the past is not the same as the prediction of the future on its own terms.

While a science predicts future events in terms of the past it is said to be an extinct science. A live science on the other hand, with which we are concerned here, makes possible the prediction of future events which have nothing in common with the past. It is said to be live rather than alive or living because it cannot be viewed distinctly from anz thing. All things may be learned by means of this science and outside of the involvement with things it does not exist.

Time is eternal. A view of time as a passage of events is limited. The difference between things which are limited and things which are unlimited is merely a limit, and nothing else.

The live science can never deal with things which are limited. Therefore it concerns itself with time as it is, which is to say eternal, and not with time as it must be. The future and the past, in the case of eternal time, are both of a common origin. In the case of limited time however the past originates and the future does not.

The present is always a product of the future and the past. Therefore we differentiate between the eternal present and that which is somehow limited. The eternal present is called love.

All things are eternally present. Whether or not they are viewed as such depends solely on man. The live science not only makes available the knowledge of eternal things but always and at the same time it improves the senses in such a way that they may more readily perceive things as they are eternally present.

In order to predict the original future it is necessary to incorporate both that which occurs by chance and also that which might possibly occur. There is no such thing as an inevitable order.

The reasons for predicting the original and the limited future are quite opposite. In the latter case a relative state of uncertainty is temporarily alleviated. The original future however is predicted for the sake of more appropriate action.

Thought may be pure and perfectly true. When it is, the difference between the future and the past is without meaning. All physical things then are alive and all events are real. Imagination is no less factual than historical deeds.

The process of thought, when thought is pure and perfectly true, is neither abrupt nor continuous, but both. Consequently a choice between the two is possible. To choose one or the other means to compromise the perception of life.

Life alone cannot be divided, neither in body, nor in the mind. Whatever is attributed to life must pertain to it wholly. Life is holy.

Live science is able to predict all that which pertains to life. This include its cessation. Prediction is the inherent purpose of all and every science. Extinct science predicts only apparent things, but never those which are merely apparent. Live science on the other hand predicts only those things which are real, whether or not they appear and even if they merely appear. An extinct science therefore cannot predict its own extinction, because that fact is never apparent. The live science on the other hand must have begun before it can be certain of itself as such, since reality cannot be divorced from action.

To date there is no live science.

End of the Science of Science

* * *

The Science of Life

Only one reason can be found for the pursuit of science, and that is the increase of life. Science is knowledge for the sake of understanding. When life is understood it is eternal. The science of life therefore achieves directly such life which does not come to an end.

There is no central force of life and no basic substance of life. Whatever lives does so entirely from within itself. It is impossible to conceive of life as an entity in itself. When something lives therefore it cannot point at something else and call it life, but it will be one with all other living things and can never separate itself from them.

Life thrives because of death and in order to overcome it. The purpose of life is more life, but death has no purpose. It merely happens. Whenever it happens life seeks the opportunity to begin. This does not mean that death is in any way or manner connected with the commencement of life. It simply concurs with it.

When life appears it is light. Light exists in the presence of darkness and darkness is not the absence of light but its contrast. It is in darkness that life presents itself, but in the light it is born. Both in the case of darkness and in the instance of light, however, life appears and is real.

When life is proven it is the truth. In the absence of truth there can be no falsehood. It is for this reason that a lie may long go unnoticed. Only the human being among living beings is capable of truth, but even without the truth the human being is nevertheless unique, because he is always at least tried.

When life is viewed it is the way. How something happens, in this way or that way, and how it is done or experienced is the same. Only one way of life can lead to the destination of each living thing. Once life has been viewed and the way discovered, the absurdity of an abstracted method and the impracticality of a permanent technique become obvious.

When life is expressed as a unity of thought and feeling it is the word. The word is not a means of communication, but it is the word itself which communicates. Whether it is spoken or written, heard or seen, the word is the same as a reality of communication. It cannot be studied.

*

The smallest possible unit of life is the cell. It is called a unit because it can exist and live by itself. This means that it does not first need to separate itself off from all other things, by means of the law, before it can come into being, but that it can be as it is, in perfect unity with all living things.

It only seems contradictory that something which can live by itself should need to be in perfect union with all other living things. In fact it is not. Total self-awareness cannot occur except in union with all living things and it is due to total self-awareness that a being can live entirely on its own terms. The apparent contradiction is a prerequisite illusion of death. Without this illusion, life could never increase and no being could ever increase its life.

The difference between being or existing and living is the same as the difference between the law, according to which life can be lived, and life itself, which may be lived on its own terms. The smallest unit of life is the cell. According to the law, such a cell can never be viewed independently but it will always, by necessity, entail the consideration of a potentially infinite number of similar cells, not one of which can be finally and ultimately distinguished from all others, since the law presupposes the denial of all that which is peculiar and proper to every individual thing. Without this denial the law would never come into existence, and without the law this denial of peculiarities and individual properties could never be understood. The extinct sciences all attempt to understand the law. A living science however, such as is being practiced here, re-establishes the affirmation of peculiarities and individual properties on an original basis, not in spite of or in opposition to the law, but in agreement with it and to the fullest extent of the law, and then beyond it into the realm of truth and individual distinction

An important difference then between the extinct and the living science is that the former questions the law whereas the latter does not.

*

The smallest possible unit of existence or being is a being, such as a human being, an animal, a plant, a rock, a flame, or an amount of water. Beings are alive, but they cannot live. In order to be alive, however, they must be assimilated. This again seems contradictory, to state first that beings are alive, and then to suggest that they also might not be alive. But the contradiction is again merely superficial, and for the same reason as in the case of the cell. A being which is not being assimilated does not exist. Since it is possible to regard a being in assimilation, it is also possible to imagine it outside of that process. Such an image however is false. It pretends to be what cannot be. The problem of the being in process, which problem is basic to all growth in which knowledge is involved, may only be solved in the direction of total assimilation, so that the being becomes the process and undergoes change entirely. The concatenation of essence and existence therefore is different depending on the point previous to the entire change of the being at which one chooses to take it up for the sake of analysis. Since an infinite number of such points can be approached, because a process remains immense, the concatenation of essence and existence can never be finally drawn up, and every attempt to achieve this end serves only to allay a private frustration.

The living science does not at all attempt an analysis of essence and existence previous to the entire change of the being into process, but instead it allows us to understand the change. The being becomes cellular.

This is not to say that the being turns into a cell or into cells. Since cells live they also exist, which is to say that they coexist, and it is because of this coexistence that the assimilation of beings may proceed. If there were no cells, beings would by necessity have to remain what they are, which is inconceivable.

*

The smallest unit of living substance, depending on whether it is seen, used or stored, is the pigment, the element or the moment. No causal relationship exists between these units of substance and between the fact that they are seen, used or stored. It is essential to this living substance that it is either seen or used or stored or not at all.

A contradiction here seems to be that this substance is living and that it can also be conceived not to be. How can life be completely negated? What is stronger, greater of perhaps more real than life? The answer is, that it lies in the power of life to deny and to negate itself, and that it is impossible to conceive of such a thing. When a fact cannot be understood it may be treated as substance. The fact of the self-deniability of life, being inconceivable, must therefore be a pure substance, else it could never quite rise above itself, and since it is also incomprehensible, as any attempt to comprehend it will demonstrate, this pure substance must be the living substance which is either seen, used or stored, else it would not be acceptable. That it is acceptable, and therefore at least a fact, has here and now been demonstrated and can not any more be doubted.

*

The smallest unit of living matter is a body. All matter has the appearance of substance without being in any way truly substantial, and therefore all bodies seem to be alike, whereas in fact they have nothing in common. Nor are they in the possession of anything whereby they can be differentiated from each other. The mistake has often been made of considering bodies to be the basis of reality. This can only happen to the degree that reality is judged according to appearances. Bodies can never be a true basis or foundation of any sort, but only a false one. Matter must always be understood as a substitute for substance. In the absence of substance, since reality must at least appear, matter goes through the motions, so to speak, of reality, and mere bodies are able to give a perfect semblance of reality. In the presence of true substance however this semblance is broken down. It occurs now that the previous affinity of all bodies, which had allowed them to adopt the likelihood of shape and form, is destroyed, and then substantially altered. An affinity of bodies becomes a relation of units of substance. Extinct sciences offer a synthesis of bodies as a material picture of reality, and they are extinct precisely because this picture can serve as a temporary substitute for reality, but never as eternal reality itself. Living science however replaces every affinity of bodies by a relation of substantial units and renders reality itself permanent.

Once we understand that matter is the purpose of substance and that the breakdown of all matter into its single units or bodies is the reason of substance, we can no longer doubt that without this breakdown, life in reality cannot be achieved and must remain a mere shadow of itself. It is of course impossible to break down matter except for the ultimate reason of substance. The attempt to do this for any other reason, such as out of resentment against the lack of truth in material bodies or merely in contempt for the falsehood of unsubstantial matter, results at best in a change of appearances.

*

The smallest unit of living material is the atom. Material is always in construction. When construction ceases, atoms, which are the building-blocks of construction, either disintegrate or

67

else are changed during a process of metabolism. Whether the case is the one or the other does not depend upon anything inherent to or related to the atom, nor does it depend upon the atom's condition or situation, which is to say its environment, but entirely on its state.

The state of an atom is final. This means that it cannot be changed into any other state. But not every atom is in a state. Whether or not it is in a state cannot be arrived at by means of analysis, nor can it be derived from the atom's behaviour, idle or under stress, but it may only be decided upon through perfect demonstration, so that the atom will either disintegrate, when it is not in a state, or else it will be metabolized, which means that it was in a state.

There are no atoms except in construction. It is not only important to differentiate between those atoms which disintegrate and those which are metabolized, but also between those which are in a state and those which are not, for the sake of an understanding of the metabolic process. During metabolism the atom shows properties which a disintegrated atom could never have had, and these are all properties of constancy. But there is no discernible connection between the process of metabolism as a possibility and the atom's properties of state as a fact. It may be observed however that the properties of state disappear while metabolism proceeds. But this is not in any way a proportion, because of the complete lack of a common denominator.

And this is exactly what material is, which is an observed duality and a duality of nothing discernible. And this is what it means when something materializes, when it changes from one into another in a way so that only the other may be ascertained. We know why this is so and we understand that it is good.

* *

The cell, as the smallest unit of life, is completely described as such. One cell does not appear to be different from any other,

68

but in fact no two cells are the same. They differ with respect to their function.

The function of every cell is determined not by the cell nor by anything within the cell but entirely by the cell's environment. This environment cannot be predicted, which means that if the cell is to function truly as a unit of life, which is to say perfectly, it must react to its environment with perfect and utter efficiency.

This reaction of the cell to its environment, if it is to be perfect, must be understood.

Of primary importance is the cell's self-reliability. It may not depend upon apparatus in order to react. By apparatus is meant whatever is not immediate to the cell.

For someone trained to any degree in the extinct sciences this is difficult to imagine. While images must be either visible or absent they cannot become part of reality. In other words, it is the custom of the extinct sciences to withhold some aspect of reality and to employ it as apparatus in order to gain the total aspect of reality. One should not be surprised therefore eventually to see the extinct scientist throw in the towel.

*

The perfect reaction to a stimulus is another stimulus. It is called a reaction not because of any inherent attributes, but simply because it follows the first stimulus. Both stimuli have only this in common, that they are stimuli, and nothing else.

A stimulus originates. It is not brought about. One stimulus cannot occur because of another. Neither consequence nor causality can be stimulated.

In order for a stimulus to occur, conditions must be ideal. For the reaction to a stimulus to be perfect, conditions must be real. A stimulus therefore cannot be brought about, but preparation may be made for it. This preparation is always conditional. Real conditions are never less than ideal. Ideal conditions on the other

69

hand are never real. The nature of conditional preparation is such that the preparation remains throughout entirely free of that which is to meet it. Any amount of precipitation, during the preparation, of an end or of a certain or particular goal, inhibits the conditions which are being prepared and they may then be neither ideal nor real.

It is impossible to decide beforehand whether the conditional preparations are to be ideal or real. Such a choice would forestall conditions and would necessarily resulting failure. That preparations are to be conditional, however, this may be decided upon, and as a result a stimulus occurs – either spontaneous or else in reaction.

A result has nothing in common with an action, no matter how closely or proximately that action precedes it. Nevertheless results are brought about. It is the mere occurrence of the action which brings about the result, and not any particularity, intention or trait of it.

The difference between the real and the ideal condition is that the real condition reflects exactly the situation of what it comprises, whereas the ideal condition reflects its intrinsic purpose. This explains more explicitly how the real precludes and includes the ideal, since a situation without at least an intended purpose is inconceivable.

Although a choice between real and ideal conditions cannot be usefully made, each condition may be discussed separately.

A condition always comprises something individual. This individual is either situated, as in the case of a real condition, or else it has a purpose, as in the case of an ideal condition. In either case the individual interacts with its condition, here effectively and there, in the case of the real condition, simply. Simple interaction, while the condition reflects the individual's situation, is not based on any rule, nor does it strive in any way to achieve or to fulfil an aim or goal. Its purpose lies in the preservation of its simplicity and in the improvement of the individual's situation, but this purpose is fulfilled automatically. Effective interaction, on the other hand, when the condition reflects the individual's intrinsic purpose, is based on a rule, and this rule is followed perfectly while the effective power of the individual increases. This depends upon the intrinsic purpose and on its conditional reflection. Therefore it is impossible that the purpose should be lost and the rule conserved. The opposite however may happen, that the rule disappears while the purpose and its reflection remains, which means a change of condition from ideal to real. The unruly effect is rejected as impossible and after a time simple interaction begins. – A change from real to ideal conditions does not happen, but real conditions need not always be introduced by ideal ones and may come about spontaneously.

The cell which contributes, during simple interaction with its environment, to that environment in such a way that not only its situation is reflected, but the very interaction in which it participates, such a cell does not improve its situation, but it changes it.

The situation in which a cell under real conditions finds itself is a product of that cell's activity. It does not reflect the cell in any way such as its condition does, but it provides for the cell a medium of operation and an extension of its powers. This is not to be confused with a tool or with a device. These can never enter into any sphere of activity without disturbing to some degree the balance of individual and environment, which remains prefect during simple interaction. The cell's situation must be viewed simply as accrued preparation which has become part and parcel of that cell and which can not be isolated from it.

While a cell is in a situation its state is said to be steady. This allows us to differentiate it from the cell whose condition has not been prepared, which cell is merely in a state and materially effete, and from the cell which contributes its interactive processes to the environment in order to demonstrate this interaction itself, and which is said to be in a variable state.

*

Every cell has the capacity for material transfer. An atom may pass from one cell to another. Cells, however, do not contain atoms. Material is in passage between cells or not at all.

When an atom passes from one cell to another it improves the situation of both cells. It makes no sense to speak of the atom's donor and of its recipient, or of its source and destination, as one might if the atom were merely an imaginary entity. In reality and ideally it is the passage of the atom which exists, and during a process, if it is to be understood rather than merely alluded to, a purpose is pursued or an intention is realized, but no attempt is made to view more than one of its aspects at the same time.

A cell's capacity for material transfer is called its material status. This status is always measured, which means that it may not exceed the bounds of the cell. But it is the bounds of the cell which limit, and therefore make possible the cell's growth. Therefore the cell's growth is a parameter of that cell's material status. The greater the capacity for material transfer, the greater also is the cell's growth.

The cell's growth may not be influenced directly, if an attempt is made to do this, the cell reacts negatively, countering such a false stimulus by another false stimulus, which results in a complete cessation of productive activity. The cell may be influenced indirectly however, through its capacity for material transfer, and such an influence may only be positive, geared towards an increase of that capacity. An attempt to decrease the cell's capacity could not be made, since the cell's properties remain inaccessible and absent in the face of a negative approach. Outsize demands can be made on it however, and the cell meets them by destroying the immediate author of those demands, and by appropriating the material which becomes available during the process of destruction. (As usual, destruction means the breakdown of something useless for the sake of increased life.)

The influence which is to bring about a cell's growth may not be measured. It is a question of making an unlimited source available, not to the cell, but simply available, and from this source the cell is able to choose freely as it requires and as it is able to appropriate and to take on. Only if the environment of the cell is uncontrolled can the cell extend its own control in such a way that its very limits increase, and not only the matter which those limits contain.

*

Bodies are neither limited nor unlimited, but simply contained. They are amounts of content. The amount of matter which a cell is able to contain cannot be measured in bodies, since a body is the smallest unit of matter when matter is viewed as an entity in itself. As content, matter is simply size and dimension. A cell therefore does not contain a number of bodies but it is of a certain dimension and size, which is equal to the amount of matter it contains.

Content and size of a cell are equations. The difference between size and dimension is that the former contains the latter while the latter contains nothing else. An equation is to be understood, and it is of no other use. The understanding itself is in the form of an equation, as when we understand that whatever is necessary is also good, or that whatever is real must also be perfect. The equation of a cell's content of matter and of its size can therefore not be any further reduced, as when we reduce shape to form and content for example, but it may be perfectly and wholly understood as it is, and nothing else may be done with it.

We notice here again how important it is to keep in mind that the human attribute is not a definition. Whatever is human is not in such a way different from other things, but it is humanity on the basis of which and in terms of which all things are and become what they are. Humanity is the essence of being.

In order to appreciate this, we need only to look at one of the many hierarchies of values which have developed in time. Usually a gradation of quality is pictured under the image of a pyramid where the top represents the unique acme of perfection, of greatest power or highest dignity and all lower levels are more and more dependent upon it, as the number which represents each level increases. Customarily what all individuals within the figure of the pyramid have in common is presented most forcefully by the top individual and least noticeably by the individuals near the bottom.

If all the universe, which is to say all things which exist and have meaning, were to be arranged hierarchically for the sake of demonstration in the shape of such a pyramid, and if no particular quality were stressed more than any other, then the one thing common to all individual beings arranged in this manner would be humanity. The top individual would be the human being, not because it is the most wise or the more rational, nor because it might have a soul or the capacity to lose it, but simply because in it the essence of being is most strongly presented, and because it presents most powerfully that aspect of all being which is human. Even time, that apparently most elusive of all phenomena, does not play as important a role and does not succumb so all-pervasively to the conditions of its own intrinsic nature as does that which we call human. Only in the case of this thing called humanity does it happen and has it happened that appearances are the same as the truth. Time is truly eternal and apparently temporary, and between those two attributes the distinction is difficult enough. Life is absolute in truth and relative in appearance, and an utterly devoted power of the will is required and necessary in order to come into permanent and final possession of that knowledge which distinguishes relativity from absolution. But in the case of humanity it is an un-shakeable fact that whatever seems to be human is so in truth, and that whatever is truly human cannot possibly appear to be otherwise. The human being is the person.

*

The size of the cell is equal to its content. This is difficult to understand only if we attempt to imagine it at the same time. If we look at a body, we can easily imagine it as a unit of matter. Whether it is large or small, compared to other bodies, is of no account to us, since we are not interested in merely apparent size. Viewed in itself however, every body reveals its size to us, which is nothing that can be abstracted from the body, and which gives the body its capacity to act as a limit.

The cell's content of matter and the body's size then are equal. Another way of saying the same thing is that the body's limiting capacity and the cell's content of matter are one and the same thing.

When two things are said to be an equation, this does not mean that no difference may be detected between them, nor does it mean that they have something in common which may be distinguished. It does mean that the two things may be viewed and dealt with at the same time without undergoing any alteration to what is intrinsic to their nature.

We have said, for example, that the human being is the per-son. In other words the human being and the person are an equation. This does not mean that every human being is a per-son, nor that all persons are human beings, nor that for some-thing to be one of these two it must also be the other. It does mean that human nature and personality are not altered or adul-terated in any way when the person and the human being are viewed and dealt with at one and the same time. This allows us to draw conclusions with regard to their origin and permits us to make predictions concerning their purpose, and it is for this reason that a living science arrives at an equation. Strictly numerical equations of course are extinct because a number, although it can represent an image, is never able to make reality in itself available. Also, the extinct concept of equality must always remain, by dint of its imaginary basis and no matter how finely the content of that basis has been abstracted for the sake of ultimate pure form, an approximation.

*

Substance cannot be measured. It either increases or decreases, not in size or amount, but simply. The cell is able to store substance. Stored substance accrues as a number of moments. The moment is the smallest unit of stored substance, and it cannot be viewed except in practice.

A moment cannot be isolated. It does not allow us to regard it under an aspect nor to approach it as a thing. It is a thing only in storage, and as such it is an imaginary entity. In practice it becomes real and unrecognizable.

Even as substance only increases or decreases and may not be measured in amount or size, so can moments, in storage, not be counted, but they increase or decrease in number. The possible number of moments in a cell is infinite. But there must be always at least one in storage if the cell is to thrive. Otherwise the cell dies.

A cell cannot survive. This helps to define the cell. The death of a cell is of the nature that does not counteract life but directly increases and improves it. Such a death which stops life or which in itself is as a cessation of life is not possible in the case of a cell. With no moments of substance in storage, a cell immediately, which means here after no passage of time, becomes an insubstantial being. Since a being is the smallest possible unit of existence, and since being, or existence, is in essence human, it may be more thoroughly understood here how it comes that only the human being, or the person, may undergo such a death which is described in the case of the cell as a total transubstantiation, when every moment of substance is realized and individuality is given up. The individual cell becomes a being, and existence is not capable of individuality.

The cell cannot be divided, but the being can. Upon division it becomes a cell again. This cell differs from the one which has not undergone transubstantiation in that it presents more life and in that is presents it more fully.

*

Instead of storing substance the cell may also use it. Then it occurs as elements. Moments are not changed into elements, nor elements into moments, but when substance is stored, it is stored as moments, and when it is used, it occurs as elements. The process directs the definition. Only in the imagination is the process determined.

Used substance is infinitely appropriable. An element is not different from any other thing. When and wherever substance is being used, elements are being appropriated, and outside of this process of appropriation elements do not occur.

A cell uses substance in order to gain power. Increased power makes available useful substance. Neither the increase of power nor the use of substance precedes the other. They happen in accord. The power which a cell may possibly gain is unlimited. This is not a power over something but simply the power to do. With a gain of power the cell's function becomes diverse, and then more diverse.

Before it has appropriated any elements of substance at all, every cell has a function which is special and peculiar. It is special in that it serves a single purpose and in that this purpose is at the same time also an end. It is peculiar in that no reason may be discovered which might explain the function and that at the same time the function cannot be perfectly understood. A merely apparent reason for the function can of course always be found, and if it is not found it is readily made up, as the peculiar history of the extinct sciences shows. But a merely apparent reason will not suit the understanding which is perfectly reasonable itself and hence, in the case of an inappropriate cell, the understanding, rather than fabricating a temporary substitute, will be momentarily suspended. (This corresponds, in the case of stored substance, to a total lack of moments.)

The cell with the special and peculiar function is unique in that is cannot support an environment. Whatever environmental influence is met by it is immediately expropriated and becomes part of the cell without however increasing its life in any shape or form. Consequently we say that the cell has a charge, which is like a burden. The effect of this charge on the cell is an odd one in that it can neither be matched by the cell by a fitting counter-effect, nor can it be rejected as meaningless. The total complex is referred to as a mutation.

A mutation is not a cell nor a being but a stage of development. The entire development of a cell is called its generation. Only in the case of a mutation, when the cell has no environment and carries an unappropriable charge, is the development itself of a cell open to inspection. One might say that mutation is the window into the workings of the process of generation.

All of generation is in essence a multiplication of cells. Nevertheless only the one observable cell always remains. In the case of the illness called cancer, the cell's generation is not complete. Instead of a multiplication of cells there is a proliferation of inappropriate cells or mutants. Each one separately differs from a mutation in that development has been artificially arrested, bringing about a state of degeneration. A single cell cannot degenerate. Only if a stage of development has been avoided for the sake of increased evolvement, which allows inappropriate cells to congregate in preparation for a regenerative impulse, can the special and peculiar function of such a cell be reversed and applied.

It is in fact the specialty and the peculiarity of such a cell's function that it may be reversed, and that by means of such a reversal of function a regenerative impulse may become available.

An impulse is either met or avoided. Whether one or the other is the case depends entirely on the totality of the cell's processes, which is its state of preparation. All of its processes must be unified and under a single directive principle, if the regenerative impulse is to be met. It is the regenerative impulse alone and in particular which opens to such an inappropriate cell not an environment, but the environment, which is the state of nature.

*

Substance becomes visible in a cell as pigment. These pigments are collected by the cell for the sake of adaptation, and as a means for collecting more pigments. Seven pigments exist which are available to the cell for the purpose of visibility.

The purpose of visibility is an ambivalent one. On one hand we need to see, but on the other hand it is not necessary for reality to appear in order to be what it is. That is why it must be understood that a pigment is at once visible and divisible.

The division of a pigment renders it neutral. But there can be no such thing as a neutral pigment since the essence of pigmentation lies in the very aspect of colour and substance. We come here to a piece of secret knowledge which has kept the epistemologist on his toes since the beginning of the world: that the attribute does not become one with the thing. The thing itself does not exist. So much has become part of us. But it has not been pointed out until now that this thing itself is the absolute recipient of attributes. (This explains also, quite by the way, the ultimate imponderability of true relation, since some of the thing must be done if all of it is to be understood.)

Substance is visible as pigment. Divided pigment is the thing itself. In the case of the cell the thing itself is life, which certainly does not exist, and the attributes of which are related to it logically. This means that without its attributes, life cannot be and that the attributes are not one with it.

There are seven pigments, and each one may be discussed separately as visible or seen substance. These pigments are not coloured matter or even coloured substance, but pure colour. They can not be separated out of the growth process unless they are understood as such. A distinct pigment is an instance of adaptation.

Adaptation is either a matter of fit or a case of matching. If a thing is to fit it must share with at least one other thing its essential trait. A trait differs from an attribute in that it cannot be separated, like an attribute, from the thing. An essential trait is one without which a thing cannot proceed. If a thing is to match it must share with another thing all traits except the essential one. (If a thing shares all traits with another thing it is the same thing.)

Adaptation occurs at a rate of speed, which may vacillate between instantaneous and protracted. Protracted adaptation is the same as a lack of divergence. Instantaneous adaptation is the same as perfect divergence. Divergence progresses as the rate of speed of adaptation increases.

The first pigment to be dealt with here is chromatin. Another name for chromatin might be simple colour. Complexity in colour has to do with the divergence of the adapting thing. No visible thing is entirely devoid of chromatin, since vision itself is a degree of adaptation of at least two things. Chromatin alone among all the pigments may be permanently affixed.

Affixed colour is the pure phenomenon, and the very capacity of adaptation. No thing is visible and without chromatin, and therefore all visible things are capable of adaptation. But chromatin, though wherever it occurs it is affixed, is not always permanently affixed.

That chromatin is affixed means that it may be conditionally abstracted. Only when it is permanently affixed however may it be absolutely abstracted. In such a case absolution is the condition of the thing itself for which the pigment has an affinity.

In both instances, when the pigment is merely affixed and when it is permanently affixed, does it have an affinity for the thing to which it is affixed. It is an abnormal condition when this affinity breaks down, and may be referred to as a pigmental fixation, which is an inhibition of basic sight.

It may be recalled from our philosophy that sight is fundamental to all other senses, and that the difference between vision and sight is a matter of abstraction. This helps to explain how a pigmental fixation, when chromatin is extant, makes possible a revision of a thing's chromatic pigmentation and change from mere to permanent affixation, or an alteration, in case the chromatin had been permanently affixed, of the pigment's affinity.

All pigments have an affinity, provided that they are not extant. Since each and ever pigment is an instance of adaptation, and since something cannot be both extant and instant at one and the same time, it follows that the pigment's affinity depends upon circumstance. How it depends upon circumstance is again a matter of abstraction. The actuality of the affinity is of course independent and definite. What is open for alteration is the factor of stability and intensity. The two are interlinked. Increase of one means increase of the other. The decrease of either is impossible. What is possible however is the instantaneous collapse of the total factor. The mere actuality of the pigment then allows it to be acted upon immanently by circumstance, and this results in a complete alteration. Any one of the other pigments is a possible alternate choice. If instead of a total collapse of the factor the intensity or the stability is increased, the affinity of the pigment undergoes a spectral change, which means that the pigment is open to influence from any other pigment, and in the case of chromatin even to the influence from another instance of the same pigment. Stability and intensity of affinity may be increased through simple practice and by means of visual art.

The next pigment we wish to discuss is melanin, which is also called black pigment. While chromatin must be present in every cell, melanin must be present in ever special or inappropriate cell and may occur in every cell. It occurs, in short, wherever a cell is totally influenced by circumstance. In the case of an inappropriate cell, this state is natural but for all other cells it must be induced.

The particular advantage of melanin in a cell is that it allows that cell to adapt to all other possible cells. Melanin is an instance of total adaptation, and an agent of pure flexibility. It operates through the use of each particular cell's penchant for unity.

A cell's inclination for being one and uniquely independent may be called its ego. It is wise to keep in mind however that the ego is not a thing but a label, strictly for the sake of quick reference. When we speak of a cell's ego therefore we do not speak of something which may be dealt with, but in reference to a complex which we have in mind.

A totally adapted cell matches every cell with which it comes into contact. The presence of melanin or black pigment in the cell renders perfect the influence through every possible contact. Contact with another totally adapted cell however is not feasible, since the two must remain contingent.

Influence is perfect when no inhibition takes place during the flux of visible substance. In order to understand more specifically how melanin operates, the various possibilities of inhibition will be dealt with in turn. All of them involve matter which may not immediately be processed because of a certain state of growth.

The growth of a cell depends upon every conceivable aspect of the cell, and on each one of its stages of development and states of evolvement. Often one of these is partially neglected for the sake of greater harmony among the others, or else all but a few may strive with especial vigour in order to allow those few to thrive again. Inhibition must be understood as a regulative device in answer to an unequally balanced growth process.

Five sorts of inhibition may occur, concurrent with the five main attributes of life. Gravity is the basic ingredient of those attributes and also the first cause of all inhibition to growth. Due to gravity growth adheres to a particular size.

The physical size of a cell is unlimited. Its apparent size or dimension however must remain relevant to a prevalent pattern. If the dimensions of a cell were not in such a manner contained, physical growth could not remain statistically free. Under normal conditions, apparent size is statistically bound and physical size is not bound; or, to be precise, it is not bounded. By statistical here is meant a set way of behaviour, which is not a law, a rule or a regulation, but a pattern into which certain processes may fit and to which they may return. It in itself is not an inhibition, but an elementary state of achieved rest. During such a state, growth is not most rapid nor most efficient, but optimum, which means both most advantageous to all parts of the cell, and least disadvantageous to other cells. During optimum growth mutual influence is at a minimum.

As soon as influence increases, generally, between individual and environment, (which means an increased charge for the inappropriate cell) or more specifically, between one cell and another, growth tends to become erratic.

Influence may be regarded as an inordinate cause of erratic growth, simply because the latter tends to follow the former. No cause of any sort however is called for in the case of influence, since it happens to be an approximate cause in itself. It is a limit concept beyond which no thought is necessary or useful.

One inhibition then, in response, during erratic growth, to a statistical imbalance, or more precisely, as a reaction to an elementary unrest, is paralysis. This is not an inhibition of motion, but of movement. Movement is apparent motion. The nature of an inhibition becomes more explicit when it is understood here for example that paralysis is an inhibition of movement for the sake and purpose of unimpaired motion. A prerequisite for this understanding of course is the knowledge that apparent phenomena contribute to real ones, and that physical reality is served by appearances.

In the case of paralysis melanin acts as a synthesizing agent. Due to the fact that the movement of the cell is inhibited, the flux of visible substance is interrupted. Melanin, consequently, as an instance of total adaptation on the basis of the cell's tendency to be one, accumulates in that cell and raises the power of the cell's ego. Only in reaction to the cell's erratic tendency to growth, it should be remembered, can the power of the cell's ego ever be raised, and never under normal circumstances. This increased power attracts the influence of all adjacent cells and creates artificially a situation of tension and stress. Tension arises out of the divergence between the tendency to be one and the tendency to erratic behaviour. Stress grows out of the conflict between the attraction of the adjacent cells and the reluctance of the cell to submit to other than normal conditions. Only consequently to the cell's reactionary behaviour do conditions become abnormal as in the case of paralysis. If new influence might be unconditionally accepted, which is not possible, then conditions would never as a result be abnormal, but only periodically other than normal. However for the reason of what follows, a reaction to new influence must precede its acceptance.

Once the accumulation of melanin in the cell has reached a certain scale and once the tension and stress have been augmented sufficiently, an electric impulse takes place and a rearrangement of the cell's various parts.

The achievement of the electrical impulse may be referred to as a hypostasis, which is a label. In fact there is no such thing, since the essence of a thing has meaning only in terms of that thing's various parts. Beyond the confines of those parts begins pure speculation. An electrical impulse is the direct outcome however of the cell's state of crisis, and a further explanation of the source of the electrical impulse is given in our philosophy.

Upon absorption of the electrical impulse, the cell is chemically valent. It should be added that the cell does not necessarily absorb the impulse. Instead the tension may be released, the stress may be frustrated and the power of the cell's ego may be spilled inconsequentially, whereupon normal conditions recur, which are immediately infeasible, because the inoperant melanin infects the cell and brings about its destruction; unless the cell is isolated and disinfected by artificial means, whereupon normal conditions prevail.

The chemically valent cell, in comparison to its state and condition previous to the paralysis, has been raised to a higher power. Only the melanin is unaffected by the electricity. The paralysis, although it instigated mechanically the effective crisis of the cell, is now removed as a mere symptom. The inhibition is therefore not overcome, which is the case when the crisis is not achieved and normal conditions are incurred through artificial prevention of the destructive process, but instead the inhibition is stimulated out of existence. However the main result of the crisis and the more important aspect of the event is the rearrangement of the cell's various parts, not now under an elementary pattern as before, but chemically under a higher power.

As has been pointed out before, no transcendental explanation or justification of this higher power is required since we are able completely to understand the resultant state and condition of the cell. Speculation and transcendence make sense only to a degree while the full strength of the cell has not been comprehended and was therefore not able to surpass itself in reality.

The chemically valent cell cannot be described, because all of its visible substance is always practically implied. This means simply that its pigment has become one with the environment, which environment, in the case of such a cell, is nature itself.

*

The second inhibition to the total adaptation via melanin which we wish to treat has to do with the cell's capacity for oneness itself.

Unless the cell is one and uniquely related to other cells it can neither develop nor evolve. Development allows the cell to grow according to is inherent conditions and states, while evolvement is growth in line with exterior conditions or circumstance. Evolution on the other hand has nothing to do with growth at all. It refers to a state of affaires. Evolution is not a thing, like evolvement and development, but a term of reference. It stands for a chaos of absurdities and contradiction in the realm of mere survival, which is a mental state entirely and has little to do with reality besides.

Evolution is unique in that it combines all the appearances of life under one false image. This false image or idol is the equality of man, and its acceptance in the case of evolution is tacit. By the equality of man is meant the perfect similarity in appearance of all individual men and, contrary to simple experience as this is, the ideal adherence of all individual men's appearances to on predictable standard. Although this false and fictitious standard can only be partially conceived and as a mere fragment, it is nevertheless held up as an ideal true and perfect, and frequently it is suggested that periodic doubt in its veracity is due to the fact that not all men adhere to it. This is like saying that a lie is sometimes doubted only because not everyone believes it. But no lie can be logically proven to be a lie, since it is based on falsehood, and those who demand a sign of their error before they will escape it in order t embrace the truth in its place will instead be given a vision of the logical consequence of their error, which in the case of evolution is an aberration human life indeed.

First we must investigate what an image, true or false, has to do with the life of a cell. Humanity is the essence of being. Imagination is the reflection of humanity. While imagination is viewed as a faculty rather than put to use as a basis of life it cannot be understood as such. In fact no living thing is without its image and no thing is without an image. Man, as a human being, is able entirely to come into the possession of his image and to transform it into the person which he then becomes. All living things or creatures are able to come into the possession of their image. It is the reflection of their individuality. Unless this image is possessed, it can be of no use to its host.

The individual image by itself however, unpossessed, is always at least false. If it is tended in its unpossessed state it may be falsified or idolized to the point of an aberration. It not only reflects the individual thing then but also that thing's dispossessed state of being. Eventually such an aberration may be infected by the hapless creature which it reflects, and then it becomes a monstrosity. This means that the image reflects the total extinguishment of being. One further stage of falsehood is possible. The dead creature is still nevertheless a creature. Consequently it still has the capacity to recreate itself. If it does not do this, it has no choice but to become part of the image which it has aided and abetted. The monstrosity now turns into a true monster which is not any more a reflection of anything but a thing in itself. It exists and takes on size. Then it approaches reality.

The process of falsehood always disorganizes itself. As it approaches reality, as every process must, it disintegrates. What is left then might be called an externality of real appearances, which may not vanish. It is preserved in a perfect state of flux, neither capable of the most rudimentary polarity or of the most elementary collection. Yet it is in order. When it becomes part of a cell it is called melanin.

The influx of melanin into a cell is an instance of total adaptation. This is in indirect opposition however to the cell's tendency to be one. Out of the resulting strife an inhibition is born which is called evil.

The ego of the cell has nothing to do with the actual state of oneness which may be achieved by the cell. The tendency is not founded on fact nor on any aspect of the fact as in the case of experience. In order to be preserved, the cell's ego must undergo a continuing strain, and in order to produce that strain, since no external stimulus or impulse is of itself forthcoming, the cell seeks out a situation wherein it may isolate itself. Isolation simply provokes strain.

The origin of black pigment however requires a situation of perfect relaxation. This is diametrically opposite to the strained isolation which the cell's ego demands. No compromise is possible, since the success of either state seems to depend on the annihilation of the other, and since no reality beyond appearances seems to be in play. Consequently a substitute reality is created. Since reality cannot exist except by means of substance, a substitute substance is appropriated, and its source is the total flux of illusion. It acquires constancy through adoption by the cell. Automatically a rejection mechanism comes into being, since the cell may not internalize what is in any way antagonistic to its being. Finally, out of the cell's tendency for oneness and out of the rejection of the category of reality which was intended as a solution to the strife between ego and influence, evil comes into being, though it has no being of its own.

The evil which inhibits a cell prevents that cell from growing. Neither development nor evolvement can go on, since both processes depend on the essential purity of the cell. The cell's ego is forced to collapse because isolation and the consequent strain are not any more possible. But the cell has now been

88

opened to influence, even though that influence ended in an inhibition of the cell.

The cell's tendency to be unique and one has now turned into a vulnerability. Previous to the ego's collapse all adjacent cells had striven to become one with the cell upon the cell's inclusion of evil those same adjacent cells are not any more attracted by the cell's ego and instead are repulsed by their own lack of ego. In reaction they develop a basic inhibition on account of which eventually the tendency to be one evolves.

The inhibition of evil initiates in the cell a neutral state. This means both that growth has ceased, and that material processes, which can never stop moving, regress. A cell in a neutral state operates negatively. The material which had made up the cell's structure dissolves. All matter which had formed the cell's initial aggregate separates into individual atoms and each of these atoms contributes to the total analysis of the cell's being.

This atomization of the cell may proceed indefinitely, since the evil which has come into being can increase indefinitely. But both must continue for a time, since the cell in its neutral condition is not capable of infinite or eternal being. When that time is up, the being of the cell has been totally analyzed and all its components merge. This is a negative crisis and may be referred to as a catastrophe. Both negative and positive components, particles of reality and pseudo-particles of the included substitute reality, merge and submerge in a nondescript chaos of infinite variety and the cell has given up its individual being.

The synthesis of this chaos is brought about by the creation of black pigment or melanin. It is the decisive substance and it does not originate apparently. The removal of the cell's inhibition of evil allows the pure flux which had entered the cell to become physical, whereupon the cell's being divides. The duality engenders a struggle. The cell has now begun to generate its own source of energy and does not any more depend on gravity to regulate its growth and to legitimize its development. Energetic expansion and extension proceeds and the new cell takes shape. It differs from the old cell principally in that it is perfectly self-sufficient and categorically in that it is wholly united and at one with all other cells of its nature.

The presence of melanin as the instance of total adaptation is now not any more a directed process but a stabilizing factor. Inhibitions of the cell are not any more possible because of the cell's extraordinary connection, on the basis of original energy, with all being, which is to say because of its humanity.

*

The third inhibition we wish to treat where black pigment is directly involved is one of the cell's appearance itself.

Whether the cell appears or not is strictly a matter of visible or seen substance. Appearance, it may be recalled, is in no way involved with reality. What appears to be red may in fact be black. It is reminded here that colour is not merely a matter of surface appeal, but that it is involved with reality. On the other hand, whatever is real may or may not appear, and if it appears it may or may not appear to be real. The complex facticity of appearance eludes the imagination entirely so that judgment according to appearances may under no circumstance succeed. If it should happen that an appearance checks with a fact, which occurs frequently of course, while the imagination is yet indistinct, then one may be certain that no reality was neither appraised nor established by any kind of judgment.

Illusion is not unsubstantial. On the other hand we know that it may never be utilized as substance. If differs from substance in that it exists even when it is not utilised, as in the case of dream, whereas substance exists only in use. It is like substance in that it may support real things, as in the case of a vision. Side by side, substance cannot be perfectly differentiated from illusion. This is the Rubicon which may not be crossed by the extinct sciences. In order to separate illusion from substance,

90

use must be made at least of the latter. If the separation is to be achieved with true ease then use must be made of both.

Black pigment allows the cell to be like any other colour. This is to say that a cell with black pigment is able to assimilate any colour in its vicinity. Since melanin is an instance of total adaptation, it is also able to relate the appearance of the cell which it inhabits. This relation is always of the nature of a likeness.

The vicinity of another cell has an effect on the melanin. Since its nature is adaptation, it is neither able to react nor to respond and instead simply duplicates the effect. This causes an intensification of the effective colour. The melanin now duplicates the intensified effect. The process of reciprocal augmentation continues until a phenomenon occurs which is called colour spoilage. Once the intensity of colour has achieved a certain height, a prolapse occurs, which means that the surface of the cell which contains melanin adopts a hue of the effective colour. Both cells now look alike. They are not of the same colour however, since a hue is merely a phenomenon to an appearance, which is a surface relation.

It may happen that the cell in the vicinity is of no effective colour. Reasons for this may be manifold but do not concern us here. The result is the phenomenon of surface tension. The vicinity of the two cells is in contrast to the colour difference. The contrast exists because the melanin is not able to bring about adaptation of appearance. The contrast, like any contrast, may not subsist however. It must work itself out.

The surface tension increases until a constant state of tension is reached. Here the attraction towards adaptation equals the repulsion of the ineffective or dull colour. Then a very peculiar crisis takes place. While the melanin continues to activate the appearance of the nearby cell, a tear occurs in the surface of that cell and the cell itself is subjected to the phenomenon called pain.

No pain may immediately be realized or suffered. The very nature of pain lies in the contrast between an apparent advantage which is to be attained and an actual advantage which is to be gained. To deter the contrast is to give up all possibility of advantage. The immediate alleviation of the contrast relieves the pain and detains the possibility of advantage. Identification with the pain, which must result in a separation of the contrasting parts, does not interest us here except as one aspect of a syndrome.

A perfect amelioration is possible only if the contrast is accepted, and a prerequisite for such a total acceptance is an instance of preparation. In the case of surface tension this is the test. The dull colour of the nearby cell whose surface has been torn must disappear and be internalized. Chromatin appears near the surface to take its place. On the surface of the cell however no colour may appear until the tear in the surface has been healed.

The inhibition which eventually allows the melanin to play its role of adaptation grows out of the nearby cell's reaction to pain. The cell either attempts to seal itself off to all influence external and internal, which is referred to as a coma, or else it attempts to turn the pain somehow into a representative ímage which is referred to either as shock or alarm depending on whether the image originates internally, in which case shock represents it as a deleterious influence, or else is credited with an external source, so that alarm creates the false image of an actual disturbance. All three of these: the coma, the shock and the alarm, are referred to as a nerve.

The nerve is the inhibition to the perfect realization of the pain. What is meant by the realization of pain may be recalled from our philosophy. Influence accepted is a simple instance of reality. Influence rejected but not reasonably is a simple case of pain. The interpretation of pain for the sake of reason and not for the sake of avoiding or negating the pain is a simple instance of pain realization. The inhibition of the move makes the realization of pain possible.

More than one cell is required of course if a nerve is to exist, since it grows out of the contrast of surface tension which requires the previous vicinity of another cell. The nerve however is not anything like a function of the two cells or of a multiplicity of cells, but it must be associated with the other cell. The nerve's threefold relativity brings it into contact with the melanin of the prime cell, and the duplication and intensification of the nerve's false or bad effects proceed where previously the cell's dull colour did not permit such a process.

The augmentation of a bad effect is called an aggravation, and when a coma, shock or alarm are aggravated, they appear as terror, horror and panic, not in that order.

The appearance of a coma, due to its aggravation by means of melanin, as panic, brings on a perturbation of the entire make-up of the cell with which the nerve is associated, and the immediate result of this perturbation is a sudden realignment of the cell's homogeneous parts according to a heterogeneous plan. This makes the cell which had sealed itself off both internally and externally accessible.

In the case of shock, which is a reaction to pain by means of an internal image, its aggravation leads to an aggrandizement of that image and eventually to horror. Horror again triggers off an exceptional mechanism in the cell which results in the entire regrouping of the cell's homologous parts according to a program of heredity. The cell which had represented the pain as an ímage from an internal source is now open to artificial suggestion.

In the case of alarm, where an external image was used in order to represent pain, aggravation causes terror through an elucidation of that image. The terror in turn causes an abrupt reformation of the cell's integrated parts in terms of a preestablished model. This model comes into being during the reformation process where it had previously been mapped out as an action. In this manner the cell which had wrongfully recoiled from an imaginary disturbance becomes capable of historic transfer.

It may sound unusual to credit a cell which is no more than a unit of life with terror, horror and panic, since these are most commonly associated with human beings. The human being is capable of sustaining them however not because it is a human being, but rather because it is human. And humanity is not the prerogative of human beings, but the essence of being. The prerogative of the human being is and remains its mastery of the universe through perfection in the world. All other beings have in common with the human being whatever attributes arise from humanity and are limited by their particular being.

In retrospect and with reference to what has been gained by the cell, the inhibition which is overcame may be called apathy. What it did gain is the establishment and manifestation of the nerve, which amounts in threefold manner to the ability for historic transfer, the openness to artificial suggestion, and the complete accessibility to all influence both external and internal.

*

The next pigment to be dealt with is white pigment or albumin. It is directly responsible for the efficient deployment of all energy and indirectly for the proficiency of all activity.

The first thing to be noticed is that the appearance of white is not the same as the lack of appearance of colour. Albumin is an increment of white light. It is also the residue of purity. Finally it is a colour and one of the seven visible substances. To be seen it need not be set into contrast, since an increment of light differs from light, which is seen or visible life, in that it partially reflects that light.

A cell cannot contain white pigment, but it may or may not make use of it. (Used albumin, which is used visible substance, is not to be confused with merely used substance, which is an extension of invisible energy.) albumin is still albumin, whether it is used by a cell or not, in comparison with melanin, which means in fact an instance of adaptation and unless total adaptation goes on, black pigment does not as such exist.

At first it is important to understand what is meant by white light. When we speak of the light we always mean white light. It is perfectly unreflected. Such light cannot be seen but it is life which is seen and appears as the light. As soon as light is to a degree reflected it is visible, can fill space, can cause things to appear and can radiate. Light in its pure state however is white, and whiteness and light are an equation.

An increment of white light is an incident of reflection. Light does not travel, because it does not go from place to place. If it did we should be able to contain it, which is impossible. Light does move however. But it does not take time to move. Its motion is instantaneous. Reflected light on the other hand takes time to move, and it does move from place to place. It may be contained as in a ray, a beam, a spark or a glowing body such as the substance.

No cell is entirely without reflected light. An increment of white light in a cell however is an exception. When it does happen we say that the cell is chosen.

The chosen cell has never been otherwise. Its relationship to other cells is always precarious, because all other cells depend upon it, in some manner, fashion or way, or even directly, whereas it itself remains fundamentally and intrinsically independent. Such a relationship can not be completely understood unless, at least to a degree, one participates in it.

A cell which contains reflected light is not necessarily for that reason visible, but it may be. The reflected light, if the cell which contains it is to be visible, must be allowed by that cell to have an effect upon it. The effect of reflected light, which is called an affect, can always be frustrated and put out. The cell which allows the full effect of its reflected light is said to be picked.

The picked cell relates differently to the chosen cell than all other cells, and if we are to understand the workings of the pigment albumin we must look at these relationships and relations separately and in their own light.

First it is important to realize that all chosen cells are exactly the same. Their relation to each other is absolute. This means that not one of these cells is able to change or to undergo alteration without affecting all other chosen cells in the same way. All chosen cells are effectively linked.

Chosen cells are capable of relationships with picked cells. The former are able to effect the latter in any way possible, but the picked cell has only a limited effect on the chosen one. In the case of such a relationship it is possible to describe how white pigment works.

Energy can be immediately transferred from one cell to another. How the transfered energy is processed, and whether or not it is processed at all, since it may also be ineffectually spilled, depends primarily upon the recipient of the energy. Once the energy has been accepted by the recipient it is called potential energy. This potential energy must then be processed in a certain way if it is to become a definite capacity, and all the cell's definite capacities, insofar as they may be instantaneously or simultaneously realized, make up that cell's power. Not until power has been expressed however, and in a real way, can the cell be said to be strong or to possess strength. It is as a manifestation of strength that albumin makes its appearance and allows the cell which contains it to appear.

White light cannot be contained. An increment of white light however may be contained. This helps to explain what is meant by an increment here, in that it is the minimal expression of a cell in direct and immediate response to white light.

An incidence of reflected light on the other hand is the minimal impression on the cell of radiating light in reaction to the cell's content of reflected light. In order that the reflected light of the cell become actual it must induce the impressionability of the cell, which is again a certain preparation.

The relationship of the picked cell with the chosen cell is one of coincidence. Since only the chosen cell responds to white light, the picked cell may not make any contact with it until the chosen cell has processed some white light. When contact does occur, it involves the activity of both cells, which in the case of the chosen cell is real, while in the case of the picked cell it is energetic.

Real activity involves both energy and white light, white energetic activity realizes energy. Real activity is based on the common quintessence of white light and energy, which quintessence of course cannot have another name. Energetic activity is not based or founded, but it flows freely from the source of all energy, which is gravity, and ends statically in a multiplicity of real things.

The involvement of real with energetic activity results in a symbiotic relationship, where both cells become one. Since both cells are open to the impression of radiating light, a coincidence of reflection occurs which acts as a bond between the cells, drawing them together by the means of magnetic attraction which comes about through the proximity of the two different origins of energy, and concentrating in a single focal point which is referred to as the cell focus.

This cell focus is easily apprehended. Once its apprehension has succeeded, there is set up an immediate relation to the flesh.

On the basis of this relation the cell itself in its entirety is transfused with new life. Attention must be paid momentarily so that the process of transfusion remains whole. That which we call the shell of the cell remains. The old life is extracted from it, by means of a suitable allocation of hormone, which renders the shell extinct, whereupon it is referred to as the cell cast. This is simply cast off. An interval occurs, during which the new cell does not grow, but it enfolds itself. During this interval no experience is possible. Once the new cell is complete, we say that it has a skin. This skin is impenetrable except to light. All light and all manner of light reveals the cell to the eye, so that it can be seen or studied. Study of the cell implements its growth; sight of it achieves it.

No two cells are exactly the same. For each and every cell there is also its specific and habitual assignation. What this assignation is can only be understood with respect to that cell. But cell and cell assignation cannot be viewed simultaneously. Each must be dealt with in turn. Only in the case of intuitive contemplation does one unfailingly follow upon the other true to life. The cell which we deal with at present, for example, limit's the function of the brain with respect to the blood. That it does this is not its use, function or activity, but that is how it is alive. The way of its life, in other words, is its assignation.

For a cell to be live, its assignation must be clearly understood. Brain cells may also be called key cells, with respect to one aspect of their assignation. Among the various brain cells again there is one which may be called the key cell, since it is its assignation per se to render all cells centrally pertinent.

All cells must be centrally pertinent before the physical body becomes available as such. All cells must be physically linked. But such a link is not easily come by. It must be ingrained via experience. Consequently this experience must be totally accepted in good faith. The difficulty lies in the fact that before it can be accepted it must be doubted. All ingrained knowledge is of this nature.

It is the doubt which renders the cell accessible, while it is acceptance in good faith – the strain following the stress of doubt – which causes the cell to be physically invested. In response to the brain cell, and in particular to the key cell, this physical investment becomes prolific and manifold potential. An interval of time ensues, during which the genus of the cell is established. By genus is meant the genitive capacity of the cell, which is to say its power of realizing substance.

The cell which realizes substance is physically sound. Consequently we are able to sense it. Its locality can be pointed out and related to the cell, which results in physical presence. This physical presence can be creatively viewed, so that it turns into agility and elegance. Agility, under the creative gaze, gives birth to true warmth and to grace. Elegance, under close scrutiny, creates free matter and sense. True warmth is eternally perceptible. It radiates evenly and steadily. A sufficiency of its perception leads to comfort and to convenience. A surfeit of its perception ends in zeal and in thrill. These two can unite habitually as magnificence. Grace is not sensible but manifest. Hence it is immediately known, which knowledge gives it feasibility as the freely given, which we can take for granted, and as the power of possession. Understanding of this knowledge renders it tangible outside. There it accumulates as ponderable attributes, which are calculated as ownership and counted as property. Free matter may also be called flesh. It is matter in that it behaves according to appearance, and it is free in that it does not depend upon us. Its easy and pleasant experience allows it to show itself as beauty and to occur to us as rest. These two may combine as bliss. Sense, referred to the imagination and to the intelligence in unison, makes up meaning and truth. With respect to the soul and the conscience at once, sense brings about goodness and peace.

There is such a thing as life which comes entirely from outside. It differs only with respect to its origin. By outside we mean all that which is not entailed by our immediate awareness. This life, which we of course cannot seek out, happens. While we cannot seek it out however, we understand that it happens at all times, beyond our immediate awareness, and as such we may contemplate its existence. As for its essence, that is not available to us insofar as this life happens, but only insofar as it happens to us. Now the contemplation of the existence of this life does not bring it within our immediate awareness but we may take for granted and given, that all such contemplation immediately goes on and does not go on other than in the presence of this life happening to us. Thereupon the essence of this life is felt. This felling of the essence of this life may be pursued. Needless to say, the above mentioned contemplation must coincide. The problem of this coincidence is overcome by sheer practice. Eventually contemplation and feeling mingle. Apperception of this life is the result. Notice that 'this' in the case of 'this life' is no contextual attribute.

Linked with this apperception there is always an impulse of abstract inquiry. This impulse is and remains abstract because it stems not from the personality but from the realm of the questionable outside of us. The inquiry is not ordered, but vague. Hence it is insisted upon. Certainty follows in its train. This is not a certainty upon which action is based, but it leads on, in itself, and quite apart from any particular thing, to discovery and invention. But here we are not dealing with discovery or invention in the realm of the physical or the mental, but always in pertinence to life itself. So for example do we discover the mechanics of the body which empower us to increase and augment our physical and mental strength to the degree that we wish to do so. We invent by the same token, via the superior force of our imagination, and in league with our sovereign fantasy, the agency of cerebral expectation, and its use reveals to us all the truth that lies hidden.

There is within us a receptive centre for the life outside. It may be pin-pointed. The name we give it is the solar plexus. Its organic function is fundamentally supplied by the ear, and the eye is responsible for the over-all organization of its stimuli. Such stimuli as approach this centre directly are always repetitive. Attractive stimuli involve the sense of taste. Memory plays its part by rendering all stimuli wholesome. So that we are able at once to touch this life, we receive it wholeheartedly, without reservation or restraint. Not only is it always suitably measured, so that we do not fear a shortcoming, to be engrossed or overwhelmed, but it comes into us with an abundance of joy and pleasure, so that it meets with our welcome.

Before this life can fully enter us, we must not only be free of resentment, but actually incapable of it. For this reason the human being will undergo what seems to be a test, but is in fact a deepening of the sensibility beyond the point of potential resistance, which is to say sense is ingrained within the realm of the elementary. One might even half-humorously say that sense is therein entrenched, and that the meaning which flourishes there is trenchant. Our imagination at this point is steeped in darkness. The mind is incapable of discernment. Only the heart full-well knows its way, and rooted in its original wisdom we find the truth which we require.

We begin with the wish that lies in all of us for our daily temporary welfare. It is a wish now which resides in itself. It springs neither from necessity nor out of a supra-personal will, but it is what it is because it is. Our daily temporary life is free of death and destruction. Beyond that however, since it is no more a preparation and a testing-ground, this daily temporary life rests secure within our eternal life, and hence it is not only free of death and destruction, but welfare is its automatic attribute.

Foremost among the details of our daily temporary life there is all that which pertains to feeling. In what we feel and in how we feel lies the secret of successful survival. This secret reveals itself in the following way. Initially we believe that we are safe, which goes without saying. Clearly we know the plan of our personal living, which is easily said. Finally are we aware of all that conditionally surrounds us, which is no sooner said than done. Our feelings do not vacillate, but they are firm. While we do not attempt to captivate all that we feel under one force of emotion, nevertheless are our feelings never uncontrolled, but always mastered.

As far as the emotions of our daily temporary life are concerned, we take full cognizance of them, not as states, but in fluctuation and in variation. Always we keep in mind that this which we call our daily temporary life is the ornamental and decorative aspect so to speak of our life as such, and that we treat it separately not because it exists separately, but so that we may focus upon it more clearly. Eternal time is not at variance any more with that time which begins and ends, but the two are really interwoven and truly involved in each other. Those who would still divorce or detach one from the other, set themselves a thankless task. Yet we are able to concentrate on one of them for the sake of a particular clarity.

Insofar as our emotions fluctuate and vary, they exist for the sake of our gratification and indulgence. Temporary happiness for example, to name the fundamental one of these emotions, is referred repeatedly to the flesh, so that an emphatic excitement of pleasure ensues. This in turn creates more temporary happiness. A sufficient degree of this happiness is presented conspicuously to the senses, which leads to a significant clarity and enlightenment, so that we are able actually to steep our senses in this equality of being with no risk of detriment.

Wherever death formerly held sway, life now moves in, in its most exquisite manner. Let us not be put off or disappointed by reminiscences of death. They are a momentary nourishment wherever life for the first time sets up its domain. The beauty of our soul for example tends to fear a blemish when it is for the first time called upon to express itself in its entirety. Human nature revolts before it begins to reveal itself wholly. Hence we immerse ourselves in this sense of revolt, so that we may be altogether bound up in this life which comes into us from without. Not our person, but we ourselves respond to this life.

Thought is entirely overwhelmed by it. This is so that it may begin anew. It passes as it were into a state of sleep. There it rests until it is awakened by love. But this love must always come from you. If it came from me you would only become confused and confounded. This love manifests itself at first as a strength. Thought is lifted out of itself to become one with this strength. Right away is established, as thought, love and strength, the physical reality of our daily living. So that it does not stagnate, it is aided by reflection. For the sake of stability it participates in the light.

The brain reacts to this life creatively. At the beginning it withdraws into itself. Due to its inherent duality, resistance meets with resistance until a stress-pattern is set up. Material is then drawn up and based upon this pattern so that cosmic images become manifest. Universal ideas are made to correspond to these images. Concrete concepts spring spontaneously from these ideas. Subject matter is in turn determined by these concepts, and substance comes about. This substance is the true preposition of this life with which we are especially dealing at present.

The brain in its creative reaction to this life relates spontaneously to the passions. This renders the passions for the first time both reliable and whole. The idol does not tempt them and the ego does not dissipate them. Hence the flesh may at once be both passionate and sound. But it is the nature of all passion to involve instinct. Precepts of mortality are not any more available. Therefore we take cognizance of the substantiality and growth-oriented permanence of our flesh, so that our passions may succeed both inwardly, as enrichment and refreshment, and outwardly, as nourishment, increase and replenishment.

The road from passion to pleasure crosses the stream of change via the bridge of the intellect. Acute vision is required to cross this bridge. It will not do to rush across with one's eyes shut. Though the passions can be fully tasted, thy can also be aesthetically performed, after the nature of a spectacle. In this way they become the universal elements of communication. Also these passions are singularly effective as cleansing agents. It is through them that we come into contact with gravity as a thing that is ponderable. Gravity, passionately understood, moves into the realm of the materially tangible. Hence we fashion ourselves a picture of gravity, and call it the earth. The earth as a picture can be treated locally and mapped out, and it may be dealt with logically as the main stimulant of our growth. It is the nature of a picture, we remember, to explain and to elucidate. This picture of gravity reveals to us, by dint of our conscious scrutiny of it, those two side-effects of gravity, violence and revolution, which have always vied with each other for the consuming penetration of all phenomena. For when a thing comes into violence, it does away with time, and the phenomenon insists on its reality. But things taken up in revolution are beyond the scope of reality, and the phenomenon undergoes extinguishment.

This life flourishes in the detail and nourishes the special. The particular and the general do not pertain to it. Neither does it satisfy the category nor does it follow the rule. Tradition today suits life, rather than life tradition. The suitability of this life's tradition is always guaranteed. History transcends it.

Here ends this science of life.

* * * * *   (1970)

104